Happy Birthday Norma.
We hope you enjoy this
book as much as we
enjoyed Dad's.
With all our love
Dad & Mom.

IN THE LORD'S DUE TIME

IN THE LORD'S DUE TIME

JOSEPH FREEMAN

First Black to Receive the Priesthood
Following the 1978 Revelation

Bookcraft
Salt Lake City, Utah

Library of Congress Catalog Card Number: 79-54209
ISBN O-88494-382-8

First Printing, 1979

Lithographed in the United States of America
PUBLISHERS PRESS
Salt Lake City, Utah

To Joseph and Rosa Lee Freeman:
parents without peer

Contents

A Momentous Weekend

When my wife called me to the phone, I didn't mind at all leaving the yard work and that hot June sun for the relative cool of the house. But as I picked up the phone, in my wildest hopes I couldn't have guessed what was going to happen during the next few minutes.

"Hello."

"Brother Freeman, did you hear the announcement?" Was that a suppressed excitement in my friend's voice?

"What announcement?"

"On TV. Have you been watching TV this morning?"

"No, I've been outside working."

"Well, listen! President Kimball has had a revelation—about your people, the blacks."

Instantly the thought flashed through my mind—priesthood! Oh, but it couldn't be so. Was this some foolish joke? I must not get excited.

"Is that right?" I kept my voice calm.

"Yes—about the priesthood. You can hold the priesthood now!"

Again the mixed hope and fear. ("Lord, let it be true!") Again my cautious reply: "Is that right?"

"Brother Freeman," came the frustrated response, "don't you believe me? There will be a special report about it at noon. Turn on the TV and see for yourself. I wanted to be the first to tell you the news."

Instant stupor of thought—instant apprehension. It couldn't be—or could it? My friend must have taken some statement out of context, or maybe he was playing his April Fool's joke a little late.

Even when he repeated the information, I kept outwardly under control. I just couldn't allow myself to get excited about his news. It was unbelievable, too wonderful to hope for, and yet. . . .

It was hard to maintain my poise when I put the phone down, though, because my wife—with her constant stream of "Who is it?" "What's happening?" and "How wonderful!"—had gotten the gist of the conversation. And certainly she was no model of calm and serenity as she danced around clapping her hands. Nevertheless, the thought remained with me—I had to stay quiet, not get excited. I kept thinking, *This is just some misunderstanding;* I feared that to believe it would produce a devastating letdown.

Then the feeling hit the pit of my stomach—maybe it *is* true! And suddenly I had to know right away. I phoned the Church Office Building and was put through to the First Presidency's office. A voice which to me sounded like an angel's spoke those wonderful words: "Yes, Brother Freeman, what you've heard is true. The official announcement that the priesthood is now available to all worthy males of The Church of Jesus Christ of Latter-day Saints will be given over radio and television all day."

As I hung up the phone, little beads of perspiration broke out on my forehead, and my knees began to shake uncontrollably. It was true! It was really true! I could hold the priesthood!

My lifetime dream of becoming a complete follower and servant of Jesus Christ had come true. The yearning desire I'd had since joining the Church—to be found worthy to act in the name of the Lord, to know that I would have my family forever, to be able to bless and baptize my own children, to lead as a priesthood patriarch in our home—this tremendous blessing was now to be mine!

Meanwhile, involved with her own thoughts, my wife (who could tell by my reaction what the incredible verdict was) sent up a whoop of joy and relief that was heard, I'm sure, throughout the state of Utah. Hugs. Cheers. Tears. Our hearts and home were filled with ecstasy as we tried to express in actions the indescribable exhilaration we felt in our souls.

After we calmed down a little (only a very little), the tremendous implications of what this actually meant began to hit us. In addition to the things which had already flashed through my mind pertaining to holding the priesthood, it suddenly dawned on me that I could now be sealed for time and eternity to my lovely wife and our three precious children in the temple. The temple! The thought took my breath away.

Our personal celebration of the great announcement was soon interrupted, however, and shortly afterward our home began to look like Grand Central Station. Phone calls came, and a steady stream of visitors arrived with exclamations and congratulations as many friends shared with us the thrill of this occasion.

About an hour after I first heard the news I was brought back to reality by a very special phone call. Those crazy butterflies started to dance in my stomach when I heard my bishop's voice on the other end of the phone. "I'd like to meet with you this evening in my office, Brother Freeman. Can you be over here at ten?"

"Yes, Bishop. I'll be glad to meet you then." My heart was beating so hard I thought it would burst.

The rest of the day went by in a haze as I anticipated the upcoming interview. But my nerves were calmed as I sat across the desk from my bishop that night. We talked about many things, including, of course, my feelings about the priesthood. And I can't remember ever having a better feeling in my life than I did after I answered the necessary questions concerning my own personal worthiness. I felt so thankful that, in the bishop's judgment, now that the priesthood could be given to all worthy men, nothing need delay my own ordination.

As we concluded the interview, I felt that maybe, just maybe, the Lord was approving of me, too.

As we talked, the bishop also brought up the subject of going to the temple. My first reaction was, "Maybe we shouldn't rush into anything. What will people say?"

"Well, I'm not worrying about what people will say, but about what the Lord has already said. If you're worthy to hold the priesthood, Brother Freeman, you're also ready to go to the temple. If you hold the priesthood today, you can go to the temple tomorrow."

"Wow!" I thought. "When the Lord moves, he doesn't waste any time!"

Two days later I entered the stake president's office, just hoping that somehow I would be able to hold on to my stomach. I'm sure I aged five years during that one weekend. There happened to be a general priesthood meeting in our stake that day, and during the meeting my name was presented to those assembled for approval of my receiving the Melchizedek Priesthood and being ordained an elder. As the hundreds of hands were raised simultaneously in a unanimous show of approval, I felt overwhelmed again. Only three days earlier my life had been so different. My concerns then had often stemmed from personal limitations which I had no ability to change. And now—now I had been found worthy and approved by my priesthood brethren to be ordained a bearer of the Melchizedek Priesthood!

After my bishop and the other elders laid their hands on my head a short while later, many poignant memories flashed through my mind: the days of learning about the Church, my courtship and marriage, the experiences of my childhood and youth—all of which had combined to lead me to this moment. Who would ever have dreamed that I, Joseph Freeman, Jr., of Vanceboro, North Carolina, would one day be found worthy to hold the royal priesthood of God!

But it was so. With my dear wife present, and feeling the influence of the Spirit in abundance and power, I received the holy priesthood and was ordained an elder in The Church of Jesus Christ of Latter-day Saints on Sunday, June 11, 1978.

It would be impossible to describe adequately my thoughts and feelings on that occasion and during that momentous weekend. I was well acquainted with the scriptural story. I knew that since the beginning of the black race, when the world was new and fresh and Father Adam still walked the earth in youthful vigor, the priesthood of God had been denied my race. I was aware that the first pharaoh of Egypt, a man of righteousness and wisdom, earnestly followed the patriarchal order of government established by Adam and greatly longed for the priesthood which normally accompanied it, but that his racial origins prohibited him from bearing the priesthood. How many other good men of the same lineage had throughout the ages lived and died with the same yearning desire was an unanswerable question, but their number could have been considerable.

I knew that after Abraham's writings scripture says little on the subject. I had wondered to what extent the primitive Christian Church was affected—probably not much, since within a generation or two of its founding it succumbed to apostasy anyway. Then, after a millennium and a half of darkness, the gospel light burst forth again, this time initially in North America, where some of the millions of the black inhabitants would in due time gladly accept the gospel message. After some initial uncertainties the principle had been set forth in this dispensation, too: blacks could still not hold the priesthood.

Like other black converts, I had recognized and accepted this position. What the Church offered me in terms of truth and salvation was in any case so far above any other church's concepts that I could live with even this limitation.

To determine the true reason why the priesthood was denied—other than that the Lord had commanded it—was something else, for LDS speakers and writers on the subject did not seem able to clearly establish a specific reason. As to whether (and, if so, when) the limitation would be removed, the general assumption was that it would be removed one day, but probably few expected the limitation to be lifted before the Millennium at the earliest.

Yet now it had actually come to pass—the Lord had spoken, and all the previous whys and wherefores no longer mattered. Under this further acceleration of God's purposes in the last days, the full blessings of the gospel would now be available without limitation to all who would truly accept Christ and faithfully follow his commandments. And I, Joseph Freeman, Jr., had now received the holy priesthood, the gateway to those unlimited blessings.

Moreover, by some coincidence, I was the first of my race to receive the priesthood following the announcement that ordination of Negroes was now permitted. Obviously that fact had no significance as regards worthiness—many of my black brethren in the Church were just as worthy as I, or more so; and many of them, having been Church members longer, had waited longer than I had for this great privilege. Yet luck had cast me in the role of a symbol, so to speak—a "first."

Suffice it to say that, after my ordination, I reflected a great deal on my position. I now held the priesthood of God. I could mentally look back over the nearly six thousand years since my race was begun and feel myself to be at the beginning of an era, so to speak. And I held the priesthood with the same power and authority as any other elder. I am sure that my black brethren who received the priesthood in 1978 had similar reflections. In the entire history of the world we were the first generation of our people to receive the power and authority to act for God. This represented a great challenge and an awesome responsibility.

These were humbling thoughts to me on that Sunday in June 1978. They frequently recur, and they have lost none of their power to move me to deep appreciation and renewed commitment.

A Country
Boy

It had just rained—and *anyone* knew that this was the best time to grab the old fishing pole and head for the creek. So with my fishing pole over my shoulder and my dog at my side, I headed barefoot down the country lane which led to our home. As I jumped from puddle to puddle, splashing mud all over, there wasn't anywhere I'd rather have been.

Suddenly my dog, who lived up to the "man's best friend" title more than once, jumped aside and sent up a frenzied series of high-pitched yelps. I stepped towards him just in time to miss being bitten by a water moccasin! Ah, country life—isn't it grand?

There's no place like the farm in summertime: the hot days and cool evenings; the smell of crops growing in the fields; the soft, warm, freshly plowed earth that oozes up through your toes. Frogs, baseball, fresh cold milk, cold watermelon—all are part of country life, and I know, because I'm a country boy.

Vanceboro, North Carolina—or at least my family—has never been quite the same since July 24, 1953, because that's the day that I made my entry into this world. With the help of a midwife—and the help of my mother, Rosa Lee Smith Freeman, of course—I first opened my eyes in the living room of the house my father (Joseph Freeman, Sr.) built—a home that mysteriously grew as each new child was born.

Vanceboro is a typical small American town—you can drive through it in about three minutes (less than that if you don't get delayed by its one stoplight). With a population of about two thousand, it rests in the middle of the rich North Carolina farmland. Our family actually lived about three miles outside of town on a fourteen-acre strip of land. And as all boys who grow up on the farm know, the country is the greatest place there is to grow up.

Professionals who study the development of children say that environment largely determines, or at the very least strongly influences, a child's personality and character development. And in my case, at least, this is very true. My attitudes, ideals, and morals thoroughly reflect the good, honest, down-to-earth upbringing I had.

My father has always worked hard to support our ever-growing family. I learned early in life to love nature and the real meaning and worth of work as I labored side by side with my father and three brothers.

Like most of the small farmers in our area (and in our state, where home consumption of crops and livestock is higher than in any other state), we produced nearly everything we ate and were almost self-sufficient when it came to food. Mother canned and bottled apples, pears, peaches, grapes, and strawberries, and an assortment of vegetables were preserved in the freezer. All of Mother's jellies and jams really pleased my sweet tooth. Hogs, cows, goats, chickens, and ducks supplied us with a freezer full of meat for the winter. Dad would also smoke lots of fish and pork in his own special way (he claims to have *the* secret recipe). There's nothing much better than biting into a ham that Dad had seasoned.

To supplement our meat supply in the winter we built small birdshacks in the snow to catch birds. Though Dad would never let us hunt or kill just for the sport of it, we did trap animals for food. And of course we hunted raccoon and opossum at night. There was always someone in the neighborhood who raised special dogs just for hunting 'coon and 'possum. We always hunted in pairs, one person managing the dogs who would tree the critters, and the second waiting with a gun to do the shooting. 'Possum and 'coon made great eating, and we all loved this kind of food. For some reason, the food in the country always seems more delicious and flavorful than anywhere else.

My favorite hero was my father, who is short but powerfully built. We worked many days together planting and caring for the tobacco and cabbage and other plants we grew. Dad had to work hard to provide for his family, so in addition to raising our own food supply, he also hired out to do work for other farmers and worked as a logger in the winter months as well.

My brother and I would go with Dad into the woods, where we'd cut wood and load it by hand onto a truck. If you happen to like using a cross-cut saw, two-man or single, cutting wood is a lot of fun and it builds great muscles. We would load the lighter woods that we could carry on our shoulders, and then my father, when he finished cutting, would help us load the rest. Dad's muscles bulged as he lifted those heavy pieces of wood—especially the heavy oak and maple—up on his shoulders and made his way to the truck. As a little boy watching his father work, I thought that even the legendary John Henry couldn't have been stronger.

My dad had proved his strength to me more than once, and I'll never forget one particular story that was often told of him. When he was about twenty-five or thirty years old, someone bet him that he couldn't lift some large sacks of fertilizer. Another friend bet money that he could. When my father heard about the bet, he picked up one sack of fertilizer with his teeth, put another sack on each shoulder, and carried all three bags a distance of a hundred yards.

Maybe you can see why I've always been so proud of Dad. As we worked together in the fields and in the woods, I gained a great respect for his sensitivity and quietness. Dad didn't have much to say a great deal of the time, but when he did speak his words were well chosen and meaningful. I found that I always wanted to stop and listen to everything he had to stay. It's a great feeling for a son to have a father he can love and respect.

I also learned to love nature as we worked in the North Carolina woods. Many times in the silence of the forest we'd hear the wood-pecker pecking on a tree, then the bobwhite would call out, a cry that was quickly followed by a mockingbird imitating the bobwhite. One by one the robin, sparrow, chickadee, and cardinal would make their presence known—or so we thought, until we turned to see where all the birds were. We usually found a solitary mockingbird providing all the entertainment.

We learned to pitch in and do our share from the time we were small children. The older we got the more responsibilities we were expected to handle. We boys had certain chores that had to be done each day after school along with helping in the woods. Every evening there would be a stack of wood about four feet high and nine feet long that had to be cut. We couldn't miss a day of cutting, because the wood kept our heater and wood stove going. The heavy woods—such as oak, gum, and maple—would keep the fires going; other lighter woods, used with a type of wood called larder (that comes from a pine tree) and boards, dead trees, and similar materials were used as start-ers for the fire. After the wood was cut we'd feed the animals. In the winter feeding took longer, because we had to cut wild straw for the animals to sleep in.

While my brothers and I were taking care of the chores around the farm, our three sisters were with Mom, cleaning the house and preparing dinner. After the evening meal, everything had to be scrubbed and cleaned so that when Mama got up at 5:00 A.M. she had a clean kitchen to work in.

It was different on Saturdays. Everybody slept in until 8:00 A.M., when the work began. After feeding the animals we boys would have to fire up the large cast-iron wash pot that held about thirty gallons of water. When Mama had sorted all the clothes, we had the chore of agitating the clothes in the pot of boiling water until the dirt was loosened. Once this was accomplished, the clothes were put in a pot of warm water, where they were scrubbed on a washboard with homemade lye soap. Still a third and fourth pot were used to rinse the clothes. This whole process was repeated until the clothes were clean.

The girls, of course, had their routine, just as we did. The house had to sparkle before their day was done. And when we finally finished washing the clothes they had to dry and iron and fold them before they could be put away.

Because of the hard work, many wonder why I call these days on the farm wonderful days, but I've always found a great joy in work. Those years in the country are the most beautiful years I remember. Some of my most treasured experiences were seeing nature in action and were a result of my growing up in such a free environment.

But all work and no play makes Jack a dull boy, and our life was not as filled with hard work as it may sometimes sound. My brothers and I loved baseball, and we played it with all the enthusiasm and recklessness that boys everywhere do. Even though we didn't have a real ball or bat, string wrapped around a rock, along with a strong stick, made for a terrific game of baseball.

Our whole family really took to music and, as is said of many of my people, we had natural rhythm. Many an evening found us singing around the piano into the wee hours of the night. Because my mother and my sister played the piano by ear, I started watching their hand movements when I was only five years old. It wasn't long before "Rock of Ages" and "Yes, Jesus Loves Me" were favorites of mine.

I gradually picked up a few rock and roll tunes, too, though my mother wasn't especially happy about it. One evening I got a little carried away with my rock and roll music and didn't realize that Mom had a visitor in the living room. My mother listened to my music for about a minute, embarrassedly excused herself from the guest, and sharply applied her hand to my backside. I took that as a pretty firm "hint" that any rock and roll music would in the future have to be played on the sly.

Somehow my older brother finagled permission to play his trombone in a rock and roll group, though, so I used to tag along with him and the rest of the guys in the community to their musical jam sessions. When they came to our house to practice I always joined in, even though most of the time I, as the little brother, had to sit in the next room.

As the chords became easier and easier I fell into the "gospel-jazz" pattern—a sort of black spiritual jazz that we all played. I enjoyed playing so much that sometimes I'd be banging on the piano at one o'clock in the morning. I'm sure my mother wondered if I'd ever quit, although she never chastised me for it. Music is such a personal way of expressing oneself that I never seemed to tire of it.

School was an adventure in and of itself—I suppose almost everyone thinks that of their elementary school days. And school in the South before integration had its own unique "flavor." Though there was a good white school only a couple of miles from home, we went to the black school nearly thirteen miles away. I really didn't mind school all that much, but of course I didn't like it all that well, either. Our school could have been a lot better if our teachers had been qualified and certified. For example, we had a couple of teachers who thought their jobs entitled them to several hours of sleep a day, so they'd put the brightest student—usually a girl—in charge and would retire for their beauty sleep. (They needed it, I guess!) I had to chuckle a little when the state began enforcing integration, because both of those napping teachers had to go back to college and earn their degrees.

I had one particularly charming teacher for four straight years who refused to let us take a recess, even though we could hear the other kids outside playing. You can imagine the result: some pretty energetic, jumpy children, and I seemed to be the leader of the pack. I just could not sit still. This teacher and I had a series of "discussions" about this, and I think I finally just wore her out.

The country always offered much to occupy the interest of a young boy, and it seems like I was always into something. And because of this it seems like I collected more than my share of cuts and bruises.

Even at the age of four I wanted to be outside with the "men." One spring day I was standing on the back of a tobacco truck when the truck suddenly moved. Being a little unsteady on my feet I fell off, right onto the blade of a plow, which immediately split my forehead wide open. My mother had learned long before how to deal with country emergencies, and she patched me up as good as new. And if that didn't leave me with a noticeable enough scar, a year later I mapped out a race course through our house. This course led me—on

12

my tricycle—to the seven back-porch steps, where I would "burn rubber" and skid to a stop just in time—*before* I'd go down the stairs. Great fun—or at least it was until one day my vehicle decided to obey the law of gravity, and deposited me—head first—at the bottom of the steps.

My mishaps were not, unfortunately, confined to my thick head. I'll never forget one warm summer evening after our family had been peeling fruit most of the day. We sat down to do one of our favorite things—eat. A red, juicy watermelon was fair reward for a long day's work. After finishing my portion, I decided to play with the knife we'd used to cut the melon. I seemed to get a real kick out of sticking the knife into the rind, making little pools of water develop inside the melon. As fate would have it, I was in the process of ignoring a warning to put the lathe away when I felt it slip from my hand and split open my little finger. There's nothing more humiliating than hearing "I told you so"—especially when you're in pain. It seems that my head mended much better than my finger—the muscle in that little finger still doesn't move very well.

Although I brought many of these mishaps on myself, living in the country comes with some "built-in" dangers of its own. I already mentioned my chance meeting with the water moccasin in the mud puddle. Another time I came very close to making friends with a snake. One evening I was working late, helping a friend of mine gather from the barns the tobacco leaves which were already cured. I entered one barn that hadn't been used for several weeks. The heat had been turned off during that length of time, and it was very cool inside. I stepped inside the barn, and though I couldn't see very well because the sun had set, I grabbed the ladder and started climbing. I had one of the shocks of my life when, as I climbed up the ladder, I put my hand right next to the biggest snake I'd ever seen, wrapped around the ladder. I did a great stunt-man jump from the ladder, yelling all the time for help. We killed the snake, and all was well, but my heart didn't seem to slow down for two days.

The first fourteen years of my life were full of incidents such as these. My activities revolved around home and family, and as I look back I wouldn't trade my boyhood for any other. Singing around the piano; walking barefoot through the fields; biting into a cured ham; drinking ice cold milk after a hot afternoon; "hitting" a home run with my string baseball; loading my pockets with crickets and toads to be smuggled into my bedroom; walking through the puddles on our little country lane. Even today part of my heart is there—I'm still a country boy!

The Holiness
Faith

Feeding the chickens and hogs and filling the wash pot on Saturday were not nearly as important as what took place on Sunday—the Sabbath seldom passed without the freshly scrubbed and neatly dressed Freemans in church. One of my mother's and father's greatest concerns was that we were reared to believe in and follow the teachings of Jesus Christ. During this part of my life my black heritage meshed with the religious roots my parents gave me to bring about perhaps the most long-reaching influence on my life.

With his classic *Roots*, Alex Haley sparked renewed interest and appreciation in the rich and unique cultural heritage that American Negroes have. Like many blacks, my ancestral roots are in Africa, where my forebears were captured and brought to America as slaves. Religiously, my family sends its roots deep into the Holiness faith, the religion I belonged to as I grew up. My mother's ministerial position in our church further emphasized the gospel teachings I learned as a boy. Now that I am a member of The Church of Jesus Christ of Latter-day Saints, it is amazing for me to look back at those who have come before me. I can't help but feel that my membership in the

Church is closely related to the strong religious upbringing that I had, which in turn is closely tied to the religious orientation of my slave ancestors. And slave tendencies, practices, and characteristics are distinctly African in origin. Because religion has played such an overwhelming role in all my life, it's interesting to see how religion among many slaves, including my own relatives, came about.

The role of religion in tribal Africa was all-encompassing; all life centered around it. In Africa the priest held a position of highest respect in his tribe, and his realm in the fields of religion and medicine was specific and unquestioned. This system carried over to the slaves in the American plantation system, and accordingly the priest (or the one regarded as such) immediately became an all-important figure who explained the supernatural and who comforted the afflicted.

In the early days of slavery, slaves weren't permitted to assemble together or to learn to read, because whites feared these two practices would encourage insurrection. But gradually many slaveowners relaxed their stringent controls, finding that religious gatherings tended to calm and soothe the slave population. So the slaves began to gather in the woods where they poured out their hearts, through word and song, to the Lord. In this way the seeds of the Holiness movement were sown during the time of slavery in the deep South.

Gradually, as reading was allowed, the Bible provided the natural text. As they read the scriptures, slaves found words of comfort and hope in a better world beyond the present. Hence, the development of a unique black church, and the accompanying almost inherent spirituality of Negro slaves became one of their most significant techniques of survival in the slave system.

Developing hand in hand with the growth of slave religion was the distinct style of music known today as Negro spirituals—religious expressions of a people who could not escape the restrictions and dominations of a strange world. These musical pleadings embodied the joy and sorrow, the hope and despair, the pathos and aspirations of a newly transplanted people. Clearly the spirituals were songs of the soul, songs that became a unique part of Negro worship.

Though this Negro church which developed within the confines of slavery had no specific organization, it was a faith that grew from the need of an enslaved people who sang songs of worship and who expressed their love for the Lord.

It wasn't necessary in the slaves' worship that they understand a great deal of doctrine, for they did comprehend that Christ's death was for their benefit. Whatever hardships and inequalities they faced in their lives—whether it was watching a husband strapped to the whipping post, the pain of the whip searing their own hearts; feeling the agony of a child being sold to another plantation, gone forever; or being hunted like animals during a desperate escape attempt—all of this was made more bearable with the comforting knowledge that the Lord loved them and that righteous works would "save" them from similar hardships and injustice in the world to come. Belief in a God greater than man was all that offered relief. The basis for slave worship was a sound one: they *wanted* to believe in God; they *wanted* to feel his Spirit direct them. This desire, added to the despair they felt, made them often susceptible to the workings of the Spirit.

In the religious celebrations of the Negro slaves, their reason and emotion, their minds and bodies, were fully joined. When they embraced the Christian message they often shouted out loud with joy. The ecstasy of such moments, repeated often in prayer meetings and revivals, represented perhaps not a flight from reality but a celebration of the discovery of strength to overcome their trials. I recall reading of the experience—which is typical—of one woman, a field-hand often whipped by her South Carolina plantation owner, who exemplified her belief in God and the strength that belief gave her. This woman's daughter said that every night her mother would

> pray for de Lord to get her and her chillen out of de place. One day she plowin' in de cotton field. All sudden like she let out big yell. Den she start singin' and a-shoutin' and a-hollerin'. Den it seems she plow all de harder. When she come home, Marse Jim's mammy says: "What all dat goin' on in de field?". ... My mammy just grin all over her black wrinkled face and say, "Ise saved. Now I know de Lord will show me de way, I ain't gwine grieve no more." (Timothy L. Smith, "Slavery and Theology: The Emergence of Black Christian Consciousness in Nineteenth-Century America," *Church History* 41 [1972]: 503.)

Religious expression definitely gave hope to those of my people who lived in the bondage of slavery. These messages of hope were taught by the slaves to *their* children, who then taught *their* children, until the movement that had developed—the Holiness movement—reached my parents, who embraced it wholeheartedly.

Many stories that have been passed down through the years show examples of religious influence in the lives of my ancestors. My grandmother on my Dad's side, Jenny Freeman, was evidently a lady of many resources. (Of course, in the "olden" days everyone had to fend for themselves more than we do now.) As Jenny grew up she saw many of her kin die because they lacked proper medical help, so she determined to learn how to use nature's medicine—herbs and roots. She figured that these herbs, combined with prayer, could cure almost anything. One day Jenny's daughter became very ill and seemed near death. A doctor treated her, but her condition steadily worsened. She lost weight, her skin withered, and her body became covered with pus-filled sores. Fed up with the "help" the doctor had given, Grandma decided the time had come to take things into her own hands, so she went into the woods to dig roots and collect herbs to cure her daughter. She made a tea from the herbs and a boiling hot solution from the roots, gave them to her daughter, and began a vigil of prayer. Everyone lived happily ever after, so to speak: a day or so later, the girl was well.

Only one generation earlier than Jenny's time found my great-grandparents, William and Ellen Freeman, as slaves in Craven County, North Carolina. Though Ellen came from predominantly Indian ancestry, her Negro blood "qualified" her as a slave. She and William worked, and met, on the plantation, and there they married—or at least they considered themselves married.

The white masters didn't consider it necessary for their slaves to go through any particular ceremony to be married. Slaves were property—and as property they couldn't walk into a church or get married, nor was there a need for them to do so, according to the masters, who thought there was no need to worry about proper marriage ties among the slaves. But the slaves felt differently, and they popularized their own special type of ceremony known as "jumping the broom.'' The oldest slave, or the one esteemed as the most wise, ''officiated'' at the ceremony and had the ''authority'' to pronounce a couple man and wife. The bride and groom would stand on one side of a broom which lay on the ground, would join hands, and would jump across the broom together. Presto! They were married. This practice was very common throughout the South, and is the way my great-grandparents were married.

After their marriage, William and Ellen joined the scores of other slaves who ran from the bondage of slavery. Part of North Carolina was slave country, but another area—Brushton—was free. During the Civil War (before the Emancipation Proclamation) slaves who tried for freedom headed for Brushton, where they would join up with Yankee soldiers. Many then actually joined the Union Army, while others headed further north via the Underground Railroad and other abolitionist groups. Great-grandpa and Great-grandma Freeman ran from Little Creek, North Carolina, to Brushton; there Yankee soldiers helped them until they found a piece a land and settled for themselves. My great-grandfather's uncle, Peter Cheek, ran with them, but joined the Union infantry instead of settling at Brushton. He survived the war to tell of its bloodshed, and one of Uncle Peter's sayings—''the war was bad and the blood was knee-deep''—has become a famous slogan in our family as it's been passed from generation to generation.

William and Ellen were among those who pioneered growing of tobacco in Craven County, and they were some of the first Negroes to cultivate a tobacco crop of their own free will. We know that they supported the Holiness movement in their new little settlement, and they passed those teachings to my father.

It's sometimes discouraging to know that many stories of my heritage have been lost. Because of the havoc slavery played with families and homes, it's very difficult to accurately trace lineage. Many births were never recorded; names were ''made up'' for slaves as they came in from Africa; families were split at the auction block, at which time partners would often jump the broom with a second or a third mate; white masters produced children by their Negro mistresses, and those children often carried the surname of the white father even though they were reared by a Negro ''father.'' Then there were the times when names were recorded properly, but were never used that way, such as in the case of my own uncle, Ledrew Grant Smith, who went through life as Willie Smith. Even he didn't know his real name until we sent away for his birth certificate.

These sorts of problems have made it nearly impossible to trace my mother's lineage, and we know very little about her people. I do know, however, of stories of one of my mother's aunts, whom mother loved and visited often. This aunt gained a reputation for being a spiritualist and a dreamer. It's told that she often had dreams about someone (whom she didn't know) coming to her home. She'd even describe the clothes the visitor would wear and what he would look like. And sure enough, that exact person would come walking through the front yard—just as she'd predicted. Mom tells of other miraculous healings and spiritual occurrences she took part in while growing up. Many times as a child I heard my mother preach the ''fire, brimstone, and love of God'' from the pulpit—and what made it worse was that she expected us to live at home what she taught at church.

The whole way of life that the Holiness faith inspires was and is built upon spiritual occurrences and manifestations of faith. Mother has often told me stories of her growing-up years where the saints, or other Holiness members, lived very close to the Lord, so close that they could often *feel* when a neighbor or friend needed help or comfort. More than once her own parents would feel the need to arise in the middle of the night, prepare food, gather extra clothes and blankets, and take them—without really knowing why—to a specific person or family. Upon arriving they would find that person to be in great need, the Spirit having directed them to help.

These kinds of giving experiences, trying to be aware of others' needs, formed a basis for my religious upbringing. We were taught to love everyone. Even when whites wouldn't speak to us, or when we had to enter through the back door rather than the front door of a home, or when someone would spit in our path, my father would say, ''As long as they don't harm you, then you're okay. You must learn to love them. We are all men before the Lord.''

20

And to know of someone who was hungry or without clothing, and to then not do anything about it, was clearly not keeping the teachings of Jesus. As far as my parents were concerned, what was ours should be shared with anyone who was in need.

Though Mom had to get up at 5:00 A.M. in order to get the wood stove burning, fix breakfast for Dad, and get us off to school—all before she left for work—she was never too tired to read stories to me in the afternoon. And usually I chose Bible stories, because David was one of my heroes. And I wasn't very old before I knew the story of Zachariah and John the Baptist backward and forward. It seems that even as a young boy I was very responsive to spiritual things and I wanted to serve the Lord and be, like David, "a man after God's heart."

Mom and Dad made it mandatory that we learn to pray. Every night we gathered in the living room for family prayer. Each of us, from the youngest to the oldest, would have to pray vocally for the rest of the family. As we began learning to pray, our prayers were simple, with the "Now I lay me down to sleep" sort of thing. But as we grew older and were more sensitive to our and others' needs, we found prayer to be a direct line of communication to our Heavenly Father. We learned to really seek the Lord with our problems as well as to always give the Lord total thanks for all we had. We never doubted that we had a Heavenly Father and that he watched over each of us. Our parents made sure from the beginning that we each gained that assurance and knowledge. We all learned young that a special warmth and protection comes from seeking the Spirit through prayer.

Not only was prayer a daily thing, but family sing-alongs were nearly as frequent. We all loved to sing, and I can't begin to count the times choir practice was held in our home. Music seemed to come naturally to all of us, and we really made use of that natural ability.

At the age of ten I was baptized, by immersion, a member of the Holiness Church by the Reverend Mr. Jones, the minister of that particular congregation. Mr. Jones was a strong preacher who was "not ashamed of the gospel." One could join the Holiness Church without being baptized, but baptism by water and fire and the Holy Ghost was necessary after becoming a member. Since each Holiness Church is basically independent, practices and even beliefs vary somewhat from congregation to congregation. Though there was no set age for baptism, most children were baptized between the ages of eight and ten years. Baptism by immersion was the common practice throughout the movement.

After being baptized, I found that my involvement in our church increased. Because I witnessed and was involved in continual and meaningful religious experiences at a relatively young age, at as early as five or six years of age I wanted to be a minister when I grew up. I'm sure there weren't too many who took seriously my five-year-old proclamations. Just as other boys want to grow up to become firemen or engineers, I was going to be a minister. And I was serious. I can't remember ever really seriously considering anything else. The stories of Moses and the baby Jesus, and many others that Mother read to me, sparked in me a desire to preach the gospel. And how proud I was to see my own mother preaching from the pulpit, calling people to repentance and begging them to walk uprightly before our Heavenly Father! I wanted to be the one telling the stories of the scriptures to others. And I didn't care how many people laughed at me, or how many brushed me aside: I would become a minister.

Because of this desire, which only grew stronger as time passed, my childhood was sometimes lonely. Oh, there were great times on the farm with my brothers. But there seemed to be something about me that alienated me from many of my peers. I don't mean to say that I was one who did no wrong; I pulled my share (my parents would probably say I pulled *more* than my share!) of practical jokes and pranks. I've always loved a good joke; and as far as I'm concerned, a joke is best when you've had a hand in it yourself. But when it comes to the major kinds of sins, if any sins can be classified as minor, I really tried to refrain from anything that I felt wouldn't please the Lord. I always wondered if I was missing out on everything because I had a conscience that worked overtime. Even by the time I was baptized, I had learned that the great secret of my happiness lay in loving the Lord with all my heart. And in many instances, this cost me my friends. My peers thought I was a real bore because I tried to live the principles that I felt and believed in. But, of course, I found much security within our family, and this helped me stay true to the ideals I wanted to follow.

At this point some might say of me, ''No one can be *that* spiritual, especially when he's so young.'' But my parents were very close to the Lord and always realized and recognized their indebtedness to him. We were instilled early with this same awareness, because in the kind of situation I grew up in religion was all we had. Our joy came from the firm foundation of gospel principles—perhaps partly because we weren't financially able to base our priorities on anything else.

As a member of the Holiness Church, once you leave childhood behind you are expected to embrace the gospel more fully by ''receiving the Spirit.'' Receiving the Spirit in the Holiness Church often occurred at a mourning bench, a bench where we would kneel and pray continually, sometimes for hours, until the moment when the Holy Spirit would supposedly come rushing in like the mighty rushing winds on the day of Pentecost. At this point the individual would likely be filled with the Spirit to the degree that he'd jump up and shout ''Hallelujah.'' Some might even speak in tongues or fall into trance-like states.

I never quite understood how this was to all take place, but at the age of twelve I had my chance to find out. For several nights one week the minister in our small church in Vanceboro conducted a revival, and during the first night of the revival he called for all of the young people (meaning those around my age) ''give their souls unto the Lord and receive the Holy Ghost.'' I and others made our way to the mourning bench, not really knowing what to expect but having a good idea of what was expected of us. We were to pray and pray until we felt that our sins were forgiven and our salvation was assured.

Though I couldn't quite understand how these prayers could put everything straight in the Good Book, and especially since I really couldn't see how the Holy Ghost could fill me to the point that my feet would literally be taken out from under me so that I'd jump for joy all night, I determined to do as I had seen others do. I really did want to have the Holy Spirit with me; I wanted to do anything that would bring me closer to the Lord.

We began to pray and pray (these things went on for hours) and, to help us, our parents and other older people who'd already had the experience themselves stood around us and sung hymns, clapped their hands, and shouted praises such as "Bless them, Lord," "Touch them, Lord," "Thank you, Lord." Well, the first night of this revival passed and nothing happened—at least nothing happened to me. So the second night we began the whole process over again, hoping to feel the Spirit and be truly saved. But again I felt nothing.

The last night of the revival I found myself at the mourning bench again and thought: "This is the night for me. I know I'll be filled with the Spirit." And after several hours of prayer, I rose from the mourning bench without having spoken in tongues, fallen into a trance, broken into delirious exclamations, or having had any other visible manifestations which usually accompanied "receiving the Spirit." After these many hours of prayer I did feel a very deep and very real joy inside, but this did not cause the kind of spiritual takeover that many others seemed to experience.

Years later I would find that this joy was simply a sign of communion, and that a night's worth of prayer would not assure me of the companionship of the Spirit. Receiving the Holy Ghost and then having it as a constant companion involves a lifetime of prayer, obedience to the commandments, and consistent adherence to gospel ideals.

There was one occasion when I was fourteen when I decided I should "fall out under the Spirit" as so many others did, and I did so during one meeting. But I was fully conscious that I was lying on the floor and that I was doing so of my own free will. I knew then that, at least for me, that type of experience was fabricated, and I decided that I would never again in my life initiate an experience such as that one.

I had seen others in my faith, both old and young, be moved by the Spirit—and I knew they were sincere. And even though I had felt intense feelings of joy at times, and even though I knew these feelings had a spiritual base, I thought there must be a way for the Spirit to be genuinely manifest in or through me. And the older I got, the more I was convinced that this would happen as I prepared for becoming, and then became, a minister.

Though I didn't feel very successful in my formal attempt to "receive the Spirit," I had other experiences, such as dreams and answered prayers, that strengthened my religious convictions. I remember one such dream that I have come to understand only since I've held the priesthood. I was just a young boy when I dreamed that I was watching television alone; suddenly in my dream a great storm came upon the earth. The fire began burning on one side of the earth, and I watched as the news media tried to cover this great "story," even with the blazings of fire in the background. I became very frightened, turned off the TV, and left our house to find my parents, who were always working. But our farm was deserted. So I started searching in the hope of finding my parents to bring our family together before the storm reached us. But the wind was blowing so hard and the sky grew very dark. I tried to find protection against the elements, but of course no one really had protection from that storm. All I could hope was that there was some way out and that I would find it.

Now, as I contemplate that dream in the light of holding the priesthood, I can see that it is my responsibility to go out into the storm of life and bring the light and knowledge of the gospel to my family, that they might become a part of the great family of Abraham. Through being sealed in the temple by those in authority, this is possible if we live righteously. And I can also see that in our individual judgments we will each stand alone before God. Our lives will be as an open book; nothing will be hidden; and from the works we've performed on earth, the thoughts that have run through our minds, and even from the very intents of our hearts, we will be judged.

It is significant to know that we are a part of God's eternal family; and though we have different earthly parents, our heritage is common—it is divine. And so this dream has now taken on even greater dimensions: we must be concerned not only with our own families, but with each living soul who is, ultimately, a brother or sister. Every person has the right to know that he or she is a child of God, sent here with a commission to serve. Since I have already been given the knowledge, I want to share it with others.

The Teenage Years

What do you do when you've lived outside a country town for fourteen years and loved it, and suddenly find yourself transplanted among sidewalks, shopping centers, and parking lots? Well, for me this uprooting turned out to be less traumatic than I'd supposed it would be.

Our family moved from Vanceboro to Greensboro, North Carolina, when I was fourteen years old—and it's a good thing we did. Mom and Dad, especially Mom, had always had the desire to move to the city, and for years we'd had different experiences which seemed to indicate—to us, at least—that we should make a move.

Dad started the hunt for a new job, and when he found work in Greensboro he sent for us and we moved, lock, stock, and barrel. The move wasn't as drastic as it could have been, because we kept the farm and rented it for a small fee.

I say now that the move turned out well for the family, but we had our share of minor tragedies at first. We'd lived in Greensboro almost a week, and we were just getting settled in when faulty wiring caused the house we were renting to burn down. It's bad enough to have your house burn down, but when it burns down and leaves you stranded in a strange city, it's just too much to take! But we were lucky enough to salvage most of our clothes and some household articles, and soon we'd found another house to rent. Our family really pitched in together then and met the problem head-on. Mom told us to just wash the smoke out of our clothes and go right back to school as though nothing had happened—which we did. We'd salvaged enough things to maintain a semblance of normal life and, sure enough, after a day or two to recoup, life did go on. We learned then the valuable lesson that we were in control of our own attitudes and feelings, and that if we wanted to be happy and face the next day with a smile we would and could.

After we survived the house-burning experience (and some other minor irritations associated with relocating a family), almost every aspect of our lives improved. The different advantages of living in the city had a great influence on me, and for the first time I started to really learn in school—my grades went from *C*s to *A*s and *B*s. I entered ninth grade as a high school freshman in Greensboro, and by this time school integration was in process. Being taught by white teachers, who were in many ways much better qualified than those I'd had in grade school, was another great "first." Subjects such as French and Spanish, which weren't taught until the eleventh grade in the blacks' country schools, were taught in all grades of high school (and even in the seventh and eighth grades).

Extracurricular activities were strongly encouraged, and soon I got involved in two areas of activity: music and athletics. I played basketball for only the second or third time in my life, and then I discovered that wrestling was the sport for me. Because I no longer had farm chores to do during the evenings, I got permission to join the school wrestling team, and I dug in enthusiastically. Of course the team required a great deal of running and practice, so often I'd come home as tired as I'd been after doing the chores on the farm. But I loved it—those muscles I had developed while loading wood and baling hay really came in handy on the wrestling mat! I won the city championship in my weight division the first year I was on the team.

27

The next year I naturally wanted to join the team again, but my parents didn't see it quite my way. They felt that athletics and all the attention associated with them might tend to have too much of a worldly influence on me, and they also wanted to be sure that I didn't get too puffed up in my pride. So I didn't participate in sports again until my senior year, when they once again allowed me to wrestle. By the time I was a senior I had a hard time keeping up with the guys in my weight class, and though my record wasn't too bad I didn't do a repeat performance at the city championships.

Those years of not participating in sports were at least partially compensated for by the fact that I got very involved in music and played the cello in the school orchestra. (And, of course, I kept banging away at the piano!) But I really loved playing that grand-daddy violin, and I'm sure many thought I could play better than I actually could because I'd put my head down, and my cello and I would really rock and sway with the music. One summer, A & T University in North Carolina even offered me a high school intern scholarship to enroll in music for the summer session. But like too many young boys, I'm afraid, I wasn't all that serious about the cello, so a golden opportunity slipped through my fingers.

In Greensboro it seemed that there was a greater opportunity to make friends than there had been in the country. To a certain extent I did with my buddies the things that other teenage guys do. School activities in music and sports got me involved in many things and with different types of people. But most of my new friends were made at church.

What a difference the move made on our church activity! For two or three years right before the move we had all attended church infrequently because of a little dispute that had occurred among the members of our congregation. For years we'd attended a little church in Washington, North Carolina, where my mother was one of the ministers; but when the head minister passed away, his wife chose to be minister a man who many members of the congregation did not want as minister. A split divided our congregation in half, and since that time we'd visited other Holiness Church groups in the hopes of finding one where we felt at home and where we felt the Spirit was strong. But we never really found a congregation where we felt at home, and as a result, we children often stayed home on Sundays, though my parents still went to church.

But this wasn't the case in Greensboro. We found a small Holiness congregation that met in the basement of the former minister's home. And these people, who were so sincere about worshiping the Lord, welcomed us in with open arms.

I'll never forget that first Sunday in Greensboro. I'd never seen so many kids my own age at church, and it was certainly the first time that I'd seen other teenagers who were excited about knowing our Heavenly Father and Jesus Christ and who were anxious to be at church. In Vanceboro there were never more than one or two girls my age at church, and we never seemed to particularly get along (but do *any* boys and girls under the age of twelve get along?). But that first Sunday I was stunned to find that there *were* others who were interested in religion.

At the end of our class period, some time was reserved for each of us to share our feelings about the gospel. ("Testimony meetings" are an every-Sunday occurrence in the Holiness faith.) I was thrilled when others stood to bear testimony to the divinity of Jesus Christ and to pledge themselves to serve the Lord. I remember feeling so overcome when I stood to say that I knew Jesus was the Christ and that I knew that by following his teachings my soul would be saved, that tears filled my eyes and my voice shook with emotion. It was such a good feeling to know that other young people believed as I did.

Since I had not attended church very regularly for some time, Sundays now became the day I looked forward to. It was so good to associate with other youth in my faith and to participate in activities with them, whether it be singing in the choir, studying the Bible, worshiping the Lord, or painting a room in the house where we met for church.

As time passed I found that I desired more and more to become a minister; by the time I was fifteen or sixteen it was no longer a little boy's fantasy, but an anxious young man's sincere desire. I had often been discouraged about striving for the ministry because many had tried to persuade me to follow some other line of work—to choose a practical and more lucrative vocation. But I knew that a call to the ministry was a call from the Lord, and as far as I was concerned the

Lord had let me know years earlier that he had chosen me to become a minister. More than one minister had told me how he or she had tried to ignore this ''call,'' wanting to do something else in life. But the Lord had persisted each time, oftentimes plaguing the individual who was resisting until the choice to enter the ministry was made. Even my own mother, who knew how much I wanted to be a minister, was very honest with me as she counseled me concerning the responsibilities and demands on a minister.

Even though I had been warned, I never could understand those who ran from or resented such an opportunity. I really wanted to live righteously, and I didn't want the Lord to have to call me to the ministry by causing calamity or trouble to beset me. I wanted to willingly go wherever the Lord wanted me to go to preach the gospel. So, from Sunday to Sunday, from month to month, I waited, hoping that the Lord would choose to call me to preach the gospel.

Wanting to be a minister put a real kink in my social life as a teenager, because I thought that if I tried to live righteously it would surely better my chances for the ministry in the Lord's eyes. Oh, I was filled with plenty of mischief—just as I had been as a boy—but I tried hard to avoid committing sins that would jeopardize my chances of someday becoming a minister.

Avoiding sin is never the easy route to take—it is not usually the most popular one, either. Temptations and peer pressure, subtle and overt, became very obvious and very real problems in high school. My high school years found me right in the middle of the unrest, nonconformity, and social revolutions of the late sixties and early seventies. The drug movement was just getting into full swing as I entered high school in 1967. Marijuana was the first attraction, but smoking ''pot'' soon evolved (or should I say deteriorated?) into sniffing glue and paint thinner, drinking shoe polish and Formula 44, putting aspirin in cigarettes, and doing just about anything that would create havoc with the body. The seemingly harmless fads of my parents' generation—eating goldfish and stuffing people in phone booths— had ''grown up.'' The sexual permissiveness constantly labeled as ''new morality'' isn't so new, because the same problems existed when I was a teenager. You really weren't considered a man if you had not "proven" yourself. Virtue was not a quality that most proclaimed proudly in the halls of my high school.

With these kinds of temptations so available to me, I was lucky that my parents *expected* a lot from me. Their faith in me was the foundation and reinforcement of my own convictions to be "in the world but not of the world." They both taught all of us correct principles, and they expected us to obey them and use those principles to guide our lives.

Being black and living in the South, I of course couldn't help but be affected by the race riots of the sixties. After President John F. Kennedy's assassination in November 1963 and prior to his own murder, Martin Luther King instigated and preached the nonviolent protest movement as an answer to blacks' indignities. So sit-ins, boycotts, silent marches, and all manner of nonviolent protest became almost run-of-the-mill.

All of this antagonism between races was somewhat foreign to me because, on the whole, whites and blacks had enjoyed a peaceful coexistence where I had come from. Whereas city blacks often had to enter through the back door, sit at the back of the bus, or wait to be served in a restaurant, this sort of segregation was less noticeable in the country. Many blacks even depended on white farmers for summer employment, and in turn the farmers depended on blacks for labor. In keeping with the slower, more relaxed pace of the country, racial tension was much more mild in Vanceboro than it was in Greensboro.

The one major exception to the usual racial calm in the country was the Ku Klux Klan, which became increasingly active during the days of Martin Luther King's campaigns. Complete with their masks, white robes, burning crosses, and bombs, the Klan harassed blacks and black sympathizers by bombing black churches and other pro-black establishments. We caught the brunt of Klan activities in the country, where the Klan was more active than it was in urban areas. I've often thought that in the country Klan members had nothing better to do than make trouble for and frighten others. Their lack of other more productive activities made them examples of the saying, "Idle hands are the devil's workshop."

By moving to Greensboro we were able to escape most of the actions of the Ku Klux Klan, but we moved right at the time when the violent aftermath created by the assassination of Martin Luther King was at a peak. Dr. King's peaceful tactics were pushed aside for violent riots, marches, and other destructive acts; more of my peers than not participated in these violent protests. Remaining neutral to the cause was considered a symbol of disloyalty and cowardice. Criticism toward school and political leaders ran rampant.

But my parents would not allow us to participate in violent or critical activity. We were never permitted to speak of hating the whites—or of hating anyone, for that matter. Actually we didn't dwell on the race question; my parents were more concerned that we had pride in our heritage and respect for ourselves—respect in the sense that we wouldn't degrade or lower ourselves by doing things that were morally or legally wrong. We never really thought we were worth any less than anyone else. I'll never forget the counsel Dad once gave my older sister. After getting married she got a job working with white women, and often at work the white women wouldn't speak to her, invite her to eat lunch with the rest of the group, or include her in other things they all did together. She felt very bad and even angry at this, but when my father realized what the problem was he told her: "Don't worry about what they say or don't say, or what they do or don't do. As long as they don't physically harm you, you're still all right. You go ahead and speak to them and smile, because that's what the Lord would want you to do. And when you've done that, then you know that you've at least done your part."

When I heard that counsel I knew that many times it would not be easy to follow—especially with all the emphasis on equal rights—but I also knew Dad was right. And as I worked to develop that kind of attitude, my positive interactions with all people far outnumbered the negative ones.

During my teenage years—those days of challenges, decisions, and temptations, which were compounded by the specific challenges my black skin gave me—the Holiness Church continued to provide a stabilizing factor in my life, a life that might otherwise have been tossed and torn more severely by the winds of growing up. The older I grew the more determined I was to realize my goals, so my participation at church was ever-increasing and always substantial.

We'd attended the little church in the basement for two years when our family moved to a different house about three miles away. This move didn't make it necessary to change churches, but my parents had become a little dissatisfied with the organization of our little "basement church," so again we searched for a Holiness congregation that we could feel a part of. We found one in the small town of Ashboro, but there were fewer members my own age in this church, so my social life took an immediate plunge. Only one other male teenager, the minister's son, attended this congregation, so once again I often found myself spending evenings and weekends alone. And in keeping with my hopes for the ministry, I felt I needed to date only girls who attended church and who would make a good minister's wife. This created problems, because as I entered young adulthood it seemed that the number of those who shared my desires to dedicate my life to the church became fewer and further between.

A possible reason for lack of support on the part of the youth was the fact that the Holiness congregations were largely made up of people who were good, solid Christians and who were very sincere in their worship. Very seldom in any Holiness meeting would you find people who weren't actively participating in worship, either by singing, clapping their hands, shouting praises to the Lord, or bearing testimony. And there were certain "principles of the gospel" which the Holiness faith taught and which the members expected their fellow "saints" to observe. Abstinence from tobacco, alcohol, illicit sex, and even dancing were just a few of these. Many teenagers found it increasingly difficult to resist the new trend of morality, and many found it impossible to follow additional rigid rules of behavior. (I remember one girl—a good friend of mine—who was a very active member of the church, until her boyfriend wanted her to dance with him. She left the Holiness Church to join his church on that basis alone.) Because motivation for worshiping in the Holiness Church was not socially acceptable or particularly prestigious, those who decided to not observe the standards of the church just didn't come to church meetings. And by the same token, those who did attend were very desirous of worshiping the Lord and bringing glory to his name.

One aspect of the gospel which did appeal to young people and which attracted new members and revived those who were inactive was the gospel music. About the time we moved to the city a sort of revolutionary movement in Negro gospel music was in full swing across the country. Old choirs began adopting the more contemporary, jazzy sound. As this kind of music caught on, I found myself right in the middle of it. It seems like I always got involved in the church choir, either by singing or playing the piano.

I played the piano in the little basement church. Another man played the guitar, and together we provided all the music for that congregation. But when our family left for the little church in Ashboro, the new minister found out about our family's musical talents and I was asked to play the piano for the choir and congregation. The minister's son was an exceptionally talented organist, and together we began to build one of the best choirs in the whole city. We even used some recruiting tactics: when we practiced we'd be sure to leave the doors and windows open so that our music filled the nearby streets. Passersby would stop to listen, and there I was, out on the sidewalks among our "audience," persuading total strangers to become a part of our choir! And what a choir we built! Other churches started to publicly complain that they were losing their members to a recruiting piano player, but we weren't discouraged—our little choir continued growing, and so did my activity in and commitment to the gospel, which made me each day more determined to become a minister.

A Yearning Fulfilled

Graduation from high school carries with it an important and inherent decision: What do I do next? College, work, marriage—all are possibilities that run through a graduate's mind. My immediate decision wasn't a very difficult one—I knew I needed to work and begin to support myself. College was out of the question for financial reasons. I hadn't met anyone I wanted to marry, nor did I feel ready to take on that responsibility. And of course, my most immediate goal still was to become a minister in the Holiness Church.

I had been working for the two previous summers at Sears and Roebuck, so I started working there full time and started trying to support myself. But the impact of my decision to support myself was minor compared with what happened when I turned eighteen.

I felt that the time had come to turn my lifetime dream of entering the ministry into reality. I had consciously made the effort to live worthy of the ministry because I had known for years what I wanted to do with my life; and even though many had tried to dissuade me or divert my attention, my mind was made up. I even had one run-in with a Methodist minister who tried his best to persuade me to enter the Methodist ministry. His arguments were pretty convincing: As a Holiness minister, I would have to work at a vocation and preach at the same time, whereas he actually earned his living as a minister. He insisted also that he had a greater role as a social leader and therefore more of an opportunity to help our people than I would have as a Holiness minister. His points were very appealing to me, especially when I knew that a scholarship to attend a Methodist seminary was available.

But aside from the fact that I didn't want to be so obligated to any one religion (the Holiness faith wasn't as structured and wouldn't so totally engulf my life) I had always had the conviction that you shouldn't receive money for preaching the word of God. Even though a modest collection taken in Holiness congregations was donated to the pastor, I never felt right about taking money for preaching the gospel.

So because of that, and for other reasons as well, I declined the Methodist minister's offer and determined to follow through with my earlier plans.

So the day came. I decided to talk with my pastor about my ambitions, and I knocked on his door.

The Reverend Mr. Burnett invited me into his office when I explained what I had come for—I wanted to do whatever was necessary to be ordained a minister, to preach in his church. (In the Holiness faith there is usually a pastor who is the "head minister," but two or three other ministers under his direction share with him the ministerial duties.) He was thrilled! He outlined for me what I needed to do in order to qualify for ordination and set the wheels in motion.

Ordination as a Holiness minister was more of a licensing procedure than anything else. The major qualification for ordination was to successfully preach a "trial sermon." Accordingly, I prepared for and satisfactorily preached my trial sermon. From that time on I was free to preach wherever I was asked to.

I was really a minister! I could preach the gospel to others! Had this really finally happened to me? To say I was thrilled would be a great understatement.

The ministerial position thrust me into a new world—a world more intimately associated with the gospel and its effects on the lives of others. Though the head pastor usually took charge on Sunday mornings, there were plenty of auxiliary meetings—Bible studies, young adult meetings, prayer meetings, social organizations to help unwed mothers and orphans—where I got my ministerial feet wet. After a little experience and exposure in my own church, invitations to speak in other organizations and churches filtered in. This opportunity to travel a little, even if only to neighboring communities, was a very welcome one. I was beginning to feel like I was too old to still be at home, and the added freedom of being out and about, especially when it involved doing what I loved, was very satisfying.

Occasions like these brought me into contact with many types of people, and I started to be more aware of that great big world outside. And because my stand on accepting money for preaching did not change, I was ever concerned about and always looking for the vocation best suited for me to support myself.

After several months of preaching in our church, speaking in various other places, and still working at Sears, I knew that the time had come to leave home—at least for a while—and clip my apron strings. I felt the nagging responsibility that I suppose all young men feel to set out on my own, to make something of myself, and to chart my own course. I needed to date girls without having my parents tell me which girl was acceptable. I wanted to preach without having my parents instruct me on the best way to preach. I loved my parents very much and appreciated their example and guidance, but the time had come for me to get out on my own.

Leaving home is never really easy, though, and as I thought of various alternatives I wondered if I'd just get lost out in the real world, where every man must fend for himself. I thought about heading for New York or Washington, D.C., to get a job, or maybe asking my relatives to help me find a job elsewhere, but at this time in my life I needed to feel independent and in control of myself.

It occurred to me that I could enlist in some branch of the military services. I resisted the thought because I knew my mother wouldn't be too pleased about that decision. One of my older brothers had just returned from Vietnam, and his comments about his experience there weren't, as you can imagine, very positive. When I casually mentioned that I was thinking about enlisting, he and my mother united to discourage me.

But one day I slipped in to see the army recruiter anyway, and we talked about various possibilities. This seemed like a way that I could be independent from my parents and relatives, see a little bit of the world, and satisfy the craving to get out on my own. I still hadn't quite made up my mind when the recruiter began listing the places I could choose to go—Korea, Germany, stateside. But when he named Hawaii, I knew I'd been convinced.

"You mean I can really *choose* to go to Hawaii, and they'll actually *send* me there?" I just couldn't believe it. But he assured me that I could "do my time" in our fiftieth state. So on February 22, 1972, I enlisted in the United States Army. You know those childhood dreams we all have? Well, aside from being a minister, I had always wanted to go to Hawaii and to get rich. So I figured that I would kill two birds with one stone—I would go to Hawaii and find a way to make my fortune.

My mother was not exactly thrilled to hear about my decision. I still remember her saying to my father, as I prepared to leave for basic training in South Carolina, "Talk to our son. Tell him he doesn't know what he's doing. Talk him into doing something else—anything else—but don't let him join the army!"

But my father responded: "We've taught him all he needs to know. He's a man now, and the decision is up to him. He'll be okay."

So, with tears in her eyes, and realizing that she couldn't hold on to this son any longer, she waved good-bye. My own eyes weren't very dry, either. I walked out the door and headed down the road that would take me to Hawaii, an island that promised many new adventures, new people, and the beginning of a new life.

Delights
and Doubts

"This must be what heaven is like," I thought as the plane circled Pearl Harbor and prepared to land. The water was the most clear and beautiful blue I had ever seen, and from the air the gradations in water color that indicated the gradual drop of the ocean floor were amazingly distinct. The whole scene looked like the posters in a travel agency—too good to be true. The beach sparkled and the palm trees swayed and the native girls waited with leis—yes, those girls really *are* waiting for the island's newest arrivals. Hawaii! I don't think words can begin to describe it.

I found that my initial reaction to my new home would improve with each day. Native girls, ocean breezes, fresh pineapple, beautiful tropical gardens, grass skirts, perfect island weather, surfers—paradise couldn't be much better. And as I thought of other soldiers who found themselves in the drizzling rain of Frankfurt, Germany, or the subzero blizzards of Anchorage, Alaska, I couldn't believe my luck. I was overjoyed with my new home; it was life's paradise, my heaven on earth—or so I thought!

But the United States Army was under the impression that it hadn't sent me to Hawaii for a vacation, so the realization that I had to work and carry on a semblance of everyday life soon snapped me back to reality.

You'd think that it wouldn't be all that hard to get your orders and find out what your assignment was to be, but the army had me spend the first few months playing musical jobs. When I had arrived in July, my first order assigned me to a unit called the Dragons First-Fourteenth. I was a mortar man in the Dragons for about a month when someone discovered that my orders had been switched and that I was really supposed to be with the First and Twenty-fifth Wolf-hounds. My job changed with the Wolfhounds, where I worked in the Red-Eye Anti-Aircraft Unit. But after about three months of this, I was recommended to be the driver for the unit colonel—a full-bird colonel, as we say in the service.

As things sometimes happen, at about the same time a new handler for the unit mascot, the wolfhound, was needed; I got recommended for that, too. Having my choice between the colonel and the wolfhound, I chose what any clear-headed American boy would choose: the wolfhound! And as it turned out, this proved to be a great decision.

In Hawaii, most servicemen found themselves in the field at least three or four days a week. But since someone had to feed, bathe, and train Kolchak VI (the wolfhound) daily, I wasn't required to pack up every few days for a stint out in the "boonies." And since I was always on base, I was also given the job of managing the base gymnasium, an assignment that came complete with a private room and freedom to run the gym as I wanted. What more could a man want? I had privacy when I wanted it; I worked out in the gym all day; and man's best friend was just around the corner.

These two jobs complemented each other perfectly. After learning the ins and outs of running a gym, I hired a couple of other men to work as a crew so they actually took care of the basics. Meanwhile, I went around the island hunting for second-hand or inexpensive equipment that I could buy or trade. Even though it usually took the army at least three months to requisition any new merchandise, I could usually scour it up in a day or two somewhere on the island. My gym became a pretty popular place to be.

When I wasn't lifting weights or bargaining for a new basketball standard, I felt it my "duty" to give Kolchak his share of enjoyment. So often we'd head for the beach or jump into my jeep for a race across the mountains. I happened to have a buddy who had a little farm out in the Hawaiian countryside. Every week or so Kolchak and I would join him for our own private luau. Roast pig, cooked in the gravel, coconut, and pineapples freshly picked and ripened in the sun—sometimes I couldn't believe that I was really in the army!

I loved the freedom these jobs gave me to roam around the island and meet the people of Hawaii, learn about their culture, taste their food, and enjoy the atmosphere that only Hawaii has. And I was especially glad to have time to attend church as often as I wanted to. It seems that good fortune in this respect was always mine in the military. From the beginning, unbelievable coincidences occurred and reoccurred that gave me private living quarters. Even in basic training I'd been a platoon leader, a position that came with a private room. Now, managing the gym, I was given a comfortable room all to myself. This solved one problem I had worried about before joining the service: I wanted to somehow be able to stay close to the Lord and active in preaching the gospel. I needed a room where I could kneel down in private to pray, without anyone interrupting or maybe even heckling me. I had supposed that to be an impossible dream, and I thought that by enlisting in the army I gave away my privacy and identity at the same time.

Instead, I found myself in Hawaii, with hundreds of other soldiers, and I was one of the few who was my own boss: I didn't have to go into the field very often, and I had a private room. This was getting better every day. At that point I could have given quite a recruiting pitch.

Being able to schedule my own time, I found it easy to attend church. Almost from the first day in Hawaii I began looking for a church where I would feel comfortable. Because I had obtained an evangelist's license, I was licensed to preach in any Holiness church anywhere in the world. So I was anxious to get established in a congregation and take up where I'd left off in Greensboro. I visited several different churches, and in the process I made a couple of friends, one of whom was also a young minister. We struck up quite a friendship, and began to do almost everything together—sort of like the Three Musketeers, or Shadrach, Meshach, and Abednego.

One of the main reasons we developed such a comradeship was that our likes, dislikes, goals, and ideals were so similar. We enjoyed the same things, wanted similar types of experiences, and tried to avoid certain activities and lures of the military.

We had plenty of time for fun, and we spent hours laughing, touring the island, seeing movies, trying new places to eat, playing basketball in the gym, and noticing cute girls we met. But it seemed that our fun never interfered with our religious convictions. Each of us felt a real need at that time in his life to draw closer to the Lord, so many of our activities were based around the church we attended. Often one of us would be asked to preach the sermon, one would play the piano (usually me), and the third member of our trio would clap and sing songs to help enthuse and involve the congregation.

But as time passed, and the more that I exercised my ministerial position in preaching, I began to feel somewhat disillusioned with my role as a minister. I often felt that the Spirit of the Lord was with me when I spoke, and sometimes I even felt inspired to teach certain principles, but deep within I knew that something was missing. I felt that there must be some power that a man—especially a minister—should have to speak as an agent and servant of the Lord. This void really haunted me, for I had lived the best I knew how and was continually trying to improve myself. What could there be that I had overlooked? What was wrong with me that I didn't feel that special power that should be with me?

The whole problem boggled my mind; I couldn't tell whether I was just imagining it, dreaming it up, or if it was real. But I would place myself in the position of having to heal someone—to actually pronounce upon a sick or injured person a blessing or promise that they would arise and walk, the same as the Savior had done—and I knew I didn't have that type of power. I had often given prayers of faith while laying hands on one who was sick, but they had been just that, prayers of faith, and not an actual power that let me know how and what to say.

I'm not sure if these two buddies sensed the same type of longing, but we all felt that only our own efforts would bring us closer to the Spirit. So it became almost a weekly ritual that we would fast and pray together, usually for two or three days. Many times we'd begin to fast on a Wednesday and continue on until Saturday morning. We'd go to the church on Friday evening, usually with some other friends and the deacon in the church, and pray for several hours, both as a group and then individually. We all wanted to gain a closeness to the Lord that would almost glow through our very presence, if something like that was possible. I wanted to be able to walk into a room to preach and to be filled so fully with the Spirit that everyone couldn't help but realize that I was a man of God.

We all felt that these periods of fasting and prayer undoubtedly helped increase our sensitivity to spiritual things. But I still felt plagued by the awful feeling that, though I was now a minister, I didn't possess that special sort of feeling I'd supposed all my life that a minister must have. That feeling was very disturbing to me. Something else added to my uneasiness: I had felt for a long time the need to be rebaptized, as though my experience at the age of ten had not been enough, had not, somehow, done the job. I definitely had more than one burr in my saddle.

Finally I decided that I was going to have to take matters into my own hands if I was going to resolve my doubts in my mind. After getting an okay for a week's leave, I packed my gear, hopped into my car, and headed for a secluded section of the beach. For the next five days I fasted—abstaining from both food and drink—and I prayed. I decided that the time had come to truly humble myself before the Lord if I was to attempt to gain the closeness, the power, and the authority I felt that I lacked.

As the days passed, I literally pleaded with the Lord that somehow my doubts would be resolved, that I would know what to do to gain the strength and spiritual power that I needed to really teach the gospel as it ought to be taught. I also asked the Lord that somehow I would be led to a woman whom I could love, and who would be fit to be a minister's wife; I wanted a woman who would have as much love for truth and light as she did for me.

My vigil ended. Of course, after being away from people for a week and after striving to grow closer to the Savior through fasting and prayer, I felt uplifted. I knew that my time hadn't been wasted, but I also knew that whatever it was that had been missing was still missing. I was frustrated! Perhaps I was seeking something that only came with age, with experience. That decision—that I simply needed more experience—was the only thing that gave me any peace of mind at all.

Other than this spiritual dilemma, my life was at an all-time high. I loved Hawaii. My jobs in the army were fun and gave me freedom as well. My new friends were like frosting on the cake. In addition to the two men I had become so close to, I'd struck up an acquaintance with a sergeant in my unit who was also a minister, and he and his wife spent many enjoyable hours with me.

After we'd known each other for some time, the sergeant invited me to visit American Samoa with him and his wife. I was due for several weeks' leave, and the idea sounded great to me. He planned to conduct some religious services in Samoa, and he wanted me to go along—not only to help with the preaching, but with the piano playing, too (I would serve as the "music minister").

We finally got everything ready, and we headed for the military air terminal to catch a military hop with space available to Samoa. We didn't suppose that there would be any delay because, even though our tickets were on standby basis, the military flights to islands in the South Pacific always had extra seats on them. But for some reason, we couldn't catch a flight out that day—every plane was completely filled with scheduled passengers.

We weren't easily discouraged: we showed up the next day, knowing that we'd be off for Samoa in a few hours. But again there were no seats for us. This went on for almost ten days. Finally, with time running out, my friend and his wife bought tickets on a commercial airliner. They told me to keep trying to catch a flight over on a military hop, and they promised to keep a careful watch on the incoming military flights and be there when I arrived.

I did try for several additional days to get on a military flight to Samoa. I couldn't believe what was happening to keep me away from Samoa: each day either the flight was full, the flight was cancelled (creating even more of a backlog), or the weather—either in Hawaii, Samoa, or somewhere in between—was so bad that the flight would be cancelled. At least I was persistent—either that, or maybe I wasn't too bright.

Finally, after about two weeks of idly waiting in the airport, I was extremely discouraged. I decided that there must be some good reason why I couldn't get a seat on a plane that usually left half-empty. Maybe there was some reason I should stay in Hawaii, I thought, rather than go to Samoa. There were still many things I hadn't seen in Hawaii, so I set out to enjoy the rest of my vacation in Hawaii.

A Mormon
Aloha

"I know that our church is the Church of Jesus Christ and is the only true church on the face of the earth today!"

Those words from a young lady sitting two seats behind me on the bus snapped me out of my daydream and immediately brought my attention to the conversation going on in the rear of the bus. I turned around and sort of nudged my way into the group involved in the interesting religious discussion. At the prompting of several interested listeners, the girl continued.

"We know that Christ's church, as it existed when he was on the earth, was taken from the earth because of wickedness and apostasy. But in the spring of 1830 the gospel of Jesus Christ was restored to the Prophet Joseph Smith in the same form as the primitive church.

"We believe not only the Holy Bible, but the Book of Mormon—which is a record of the peoples on the American continents, the Lamanites, who are a remnant of the House of Israel—to be the word of God. We know that God the Father, his Son Jesus Christ, and the Holy Ghost are three separate and glorified personages who comprise the Godhead."

As the same young lady continued, she told of many more interesting concepts that her church taught. And the more I listened, the more my curiosity was piqued.

After deciding not to spend any more time waiting for a plane to Samoa, I had taken a cab from the airport to my hotel, planning on the way how I'd spend my vacation days. One place on the island that I had never taken the time to see but had heard much about was the Polynesian Cultural Center. I didn't even really know what it was, but more than once friends had encouraged me to see it. So the first thing I did after unpacking was to check the tour schedule to the Cultural Center.

Now I found myself in the middle of a religious discussion with members of the Mormon Church. I hadn't even known that the Polynesian Cultural Center was sponsored by the Mormon Church; as a matter of fact, until only a short while before I hadn't even really known who the Mormons were. I sort of thought they were the ones who wore those long coats, black hats, and who had a bunch of wives. Oh, I'd had a run-in with a member of this rather strange church back in Louisiana. All that encounter had resulted in was a heated debate over the question of baptism of the dead, which had sounded to me like a rather useless practice. My impressions of Mormons hadn't been too favorable after that experience.

But then only a month or two before my trip to the Cultural Center I had had an interesting talk with a sergeant in my unit. This sergeant, who was my supervisor, was a fast talker who liked to have his way. As we stood outside Kolchak's dog kennel one evening, our conversation had somehow turned to the subject of religion. He knew that I was a Holiness minister, and he began to tell me about his church. He had begun by saying that, even though he was an inactive member of the Mormon Church, he knew that it was the only true church on the face of the earth.

He had gone on to explain a little about his church's beliefs regarding life before this life and the covenants of baptism and the separateness of members of the Godhead. I was impressed with the feeling that had come over me when he had talked about those doctrines, and I remember thinking that *sometime* I would have to get to know a little more about his religion.

Now, quite by accident, I found myself finding out a little bit more. And what I heard intrigued me. Because I was dissatisfied with the Holiness churches I'd been attending in Hawaii, I had begun a gradual study of other religions. Buddhism had been my most recent subject of interest. It seemed to me that somehow there must be a way to link up the beliefs of people all over the world. After all, weren't we all children of a Heavenly Father, the only difference being that we worshipped in different languages and in different ways? And though I had never been reared with the idea that there was only "one true church" on the earth, the more I traveled and the more I studied the scriptures, the more I realized that Christ, in his ministry, had organized *a* church, his church; the words of the New Testament seemed to speak to a specific people, a specific church. Was it possible that there was *one* church on earth that was in fact Christ's church, organized in the same way that his church had been organized, and teaching the principles that he had taught?

These questions came back to me now as I listened to the sincere testimony of the young lady on the bus. We arrived at the Cultural Center all too soon, and I found myself rubbing shoulders with many different Mormons. Though most of the people on the tour elected to go on a special Cultural Center tour, I wanted to just wander around, take everything in, and maybe ask some questions of the guides and hostesses.

As I did so, the people to whom I asked questions about the gospel seemed so patient and pleasant to talk with. In that short three-hour visit I picked up many little tidbits of information about the Mormons from a number of Church members. Some told me about the family home evening program; others emphasized that the father presides as the patriarch of his home; and yet others explained the organizational structure of the Church.

As I left the Cultural Center that day I couldn't help but be impressed with what I'd heard. Organizationally speaking, this church seemed to be very well structured. And the great emphasis on the father and the family plus the loving nature that the people at the Cultural Center had shown really appealed to me. I left thinking that even though this was probably not the one true church, these people definitely had something on the ball.

For the next few days my mind was filled with all I'd heard and felt at the Cultural Center, so a few days later I took another bus back to the center. Again I avoided the regular tour, preferring to walk around the gardens of the center. I spent several hours sitting under the shade trees, talking to the Polynesian natives who serve as guides and hostesses, and they told me many more things about the Church. I heard about eternal marriage and the principle of faith, the great educational opportunities that the Church provides for many Polynesians, and the strong emphasis that the Church places on things such as honesty and charity.

And, as was bound to happen, one young girl explained, the best she could, that Negroes were not allowed to hold the priesthood—a priesthood these Mormons seemed to have such a high regard for. But at this point in my investigation of the Church, the Negro/priesthood doctrine did not particularly bother me—probably because I didn't consider it to be a matter of immediate or even potential concern. I was merely interested in finding out about a group of people who made me feel good inside. I didn't suppose there was any need to worry about holding something I'd probably never even *want* to hold.

And these people did leave me with such a warm feeling! One thing that never failed to touch me as different members shared with me their beliefs and knowledge about the Church was that never did a discussion end without this newly found friend bearing testimony that he knew The Church of Jesus Christ of Latter-day Saints to be Christ's true church on the earth today. These words always touched my heart, and I felt a great spirit of sincerity and truth in them.

Evening came, and I found myself still at the Cultural Center. As I was preparing to leave I began walking across a small bridge just at the same moment that a pretty Samoan girl started across from the other side. She had a beautiful smile, and as our eyes met, I said, "Talofa."

Her surprise that a black man greeted her in her native tongue was evident as she asked, "How do you speak my language?"

I responded that some friends of mine who had gone to American Samoa had taught me a few words. She smiled; we both continued on our separate ways across the bridge. But a few minutes later as I walked to catch my bus I noticed her again, this time sitting on a woven mat beneath some coconut trees. Deciding this opportunity was too good to pass up, I asked her if I could join her, and we began a very pleasant conversation.

I found that this beautiful young Samoan girl, Toe (pronounced *'Tō-ā*) Isapela Leituala, had been on a mission for the Mormon Church; the more we talked, the more certain I was that there was truly something unique about her. She told me about her homeland (or "home place" as she called it), and the way she had been reared. She explained that she had come to Hawaii to attend the Church College of Hawaii.

As our discussion shifted to the Mormon Church, she told me that she knew she had a Heavenly Father who truly watched over her and cared for her and that Jesus Christ, his Son, had died for our sins. I'm not sure how long we sat there talking, but as the time came for me to go (I'd already missed the first bus), she concluded by saying that she knew that The Church of Jesus Christ of Latter-day Saints was the only true church on the earth and that the Prophet Joseph Smith was a true prophet of God.

"I love Joseph Smith with all my heart," were her final words.

As I heard her pronouncement, I couldn't help but think, "Before this is over, you're gonna love Joseph Freeman, too!" I guess my heartstrings were already being tugged.

Again the thoughts of what I had heard—and of Toe—stayed with me after I left the Cultural Center. These Mormons had a special warmth that radiated to others, and even though I'd been told that day that neither I nor any other members of my race could hold the priesthood in the Mormon Church, I still felt this special warmth from these people.

As often happens to young men who've had a young woman catch their eye, my mind did keep wandering back to Toe. Not only was she beautiful and kind and enjoyable to talk to, but she seemed to have so many qualities that I'd always imagined my own wife should have. And she had such a love for her gospel! It seemed, at least from my first impression, that her church and her Heavenly Father were her first concerns. For these reasons I couldn't get her out of my mind.

For years I'd kept my eye out for a girl who had those sort of feelings about spiritual things, so a few days later I returned to the Cultural Center a third time, hoping to "run into" Toe. I nonchalantly strolled around for a while, but soon decided that the subtle approach was getting me nowhere, so I boldly walked to the information desk and asked if Toe was working and where I could find her. And wouldn't you know it—it was her day off! I was very disappointed; I'd been all prepared to woo her with my charms. But if she wasn't there, she wasn't there. It was too late in the day to head for some other attraction on the island, so to keep the day from being a complete loss I thought I'd enjoy talking with others at the Cultural Center—for a while, at least.

Before long I again found myself deep in conversation with another lovely young lady who happened to be a friend of Toe's—though I didn't know that. Her name was Polili Alofepo. I soon found that I wasn't dealing with a quiet, fragile girl. Polili wasn't afraid to say what she thought, and as our conversation progressed, her words hit me right in the face.

After finding out that I was an ordained minister of another church she queried, "How do your ministers ordain one another? And what gives them the authority to confer the ministry on one another?"

I sort of choked, and finally replied that I wasn't really sure and shouldn't talk about it anyway, because ordination was a very sacred matter that we weren't allowed to discuss openly in our church.

Polili then explained to me the concept of priesthood ordination by the laying on of hands, and explained the direct and divine authority related to such ordination. She asked if I had been ordained by the laying on of hands—as Jesus had ordained his apostles—and if the person who conferred the ministry on me had authority from God to do so.

"Can you trace your priesthood lineage back to the Savior?" Polili was insistent. "Do you know whether the person who ordained you a minister had the authority from Heavenly Father to do so?"

These words really irritated me, because they questioned the authenticity of my own ministerial calling. And frankly, by this time I wasn't too interested in pursuing the conversation. But before I could either say anything or politely break away, Polili asked, ''How can the Lord lead you if you don't have a prophet to guide you—a prophet ordained from on high as in days of old? In the book of Amos in the Old Testament it says that the Lord would do nothing except he reveal his secret unto the prophets. How can he reveal his will to you if you aren't led by a prophet?''

That was the last straw! Who *did* Polili think she was, anyway? I knew that the Lord spoke to me and led me, and I told her so. I had had enough of being heckled and pressured by some girl, and I was more than ready to leave.

But before I could escape, she asked if I had a Book of Mormon. I replied that I did. She then asked if I'd read it and if I'd come back next week to discuss it with her. At that particular moment I couldn't think of anything I'd rather not be doing in a week, but she persisted, challenging me to just read the first twenty-five pages. With the hope that maybe I could get away if I promised this, I said that I would and then—thank heavens—I made my getaway.

I'd about had my fill of Mormons that day, but as I neared the exit a young man named Vonu stopped me and said he'd heard I was looking for Toe. Naturally my interest was immediately revived as I discovered that Vonu and his girl friend were good friends of Toe's. Vonu was also Samoan, and had evidently served a mission in the same place as Toe had.

After we'd talked for only a short while, Vonu invited me to go with him to spend the weekend at his home. I just couldn't believe it! I had never seen him before, and after only a few minutes he wanted me to go to his home! These Mormons were something else! But by this time all I wanted was to get away from the Cultural Center and head back to the base. I'd come trying to pursue a young lady, and instead I had found myself bombarded by one. I tried to gently decline the weekend offer—and I kept declining it all the way to Vonu's home.

I just couldn't believe that I was in a strange car with a strange man headed for some unknown destination. But before I knew it I was being introduced to his girl friend and was being pirated off to two different luaus. All in all, the evening did turn out to be very enjoyable—a great improvement on the rest of the day. But the real surprise was yet to come.

Early the next morning I felt someone shaking me. After the fog cleared and I realized where I was, Vonu asked the big question: "Would you like to go to priesthood meeting with me?"

The question was actually more of a formality than anything else, because I'm sure he'd already decided that I was going with him. And though I didn't really have the proper clothes, I again found myself in a car despite my protests, and we were headed for a Mormon church. This priesthood meeting turned out to be rather interesting and enjoyable, so I decided it wouldn't hurt me to try out their Sunday School as well.

When I discovered that there was a little time between these two meetings, I picked up a *Missionary Pal* and began thumbing through it. Several items really caught my interest. My church had always forbidden dancing, saying that it was of the devil. Yet I had never been able to justify that belief with the scriptures, and had never quite agreed with it myself—as I was growing up I'd seen more than one teenager drop away from our church because of this very thing. In the *Missionary Pal* I discovered that Mormons believe in dancing.

Next I flipped the pages over to the section entitled *Godhead*. In the past few days many had explained the Mormon perception of the Godhead, that it contained three separate Personages: God the Father, God the Son, and the Holy Ghost. And though I had always been taught that these three Beings comprised the Trinity and were all one, I already believed the principle that each existed as a separate Being.

Then another heading really caught my eye: *Baptism for the Dead*. My mind immediately flashed back to that rather heated discussion I'd had with the Mormon in Louisiana. How crazy I'd thought he was! But now as I read what the *Missionary Pal* had to say about this particular practice, I could see that maybe there *was* a reason for it after all. It wasn't baptism *of* the dead, but baptism *for* the dead, and as I remembered Jesus' words to Nicodemus that "except a man be born again he cannot enter into the kingdom of God," I suddenly felt that baptism for the dead must be a true principle.

After all, what about all those who for some reason or another didn't have the chance to be baptized on this earth? What happened to them? I completely believed that God is not a respecter of persons, but that he loves us all equally and perfectly, so surely there must be a way to give everyone the same opportunity to be baptized. Yes, more and more of the ideas of these Mormons were making sense. I decided that even if they were not the "only true church," they sure did have some good ideas.

There was definitely a special spirit among these people, and I had felt it at the Cultural Center, in talking with Toe, and during these days with Vonu. Sunday ended all too soon, and I found myself reluctantly heading back to base. How glad I was that these strangers had pirated me off to their home for the weekend! It had been one of the most enjoyable I'd spent in a long while.

Little did I know that even as I was en route back to base the wheels of Mormon missionary work had begun to turn in my behalf. Later I found that scarcely had I said my thank yous and good-byes and was out the door that day than Vonu was on the phone to Toe telling her, I'm sure, about this "golden contact" that she just had to get to work on. And twenty-four hours didn't go by before Toe tried to contact me.

The first four days of the next week I was a little hard to catch, though, because my squadron was out in the field on maneuvers. I had scarcely stepped back in the apartment and jumped in the shower than the phone rang—isn't that always when it rings? And for some reason, I just knew it would be Toe.

When I heard her voice on the phone I was elated—and at least a little disappointed when I found out she only wanted to talk about the Church. But my interest in the new doctrines had by that time become something I needed to recognize and respond to, and since I trusted and liked Toe very much, she was the one to ask the questions which I'd stored up for the past few days. That night we began a four-hour vigil over the phone, and, believe it or not, we talked about religion in general and the gospel in particular for the whole time.

The next night when she called we staged a repeat performance. (Thank heavens our phone calls weren't long distance!) On the third night I couldn't wait for her to call, so I took the initiative. Deeper and deeper we dug into the principles of the Mormon Church, and with each progressive step and each new particle of understanding I felt myself being increasingly exposed to things that were true and beautiful and full of light.

Of course, my interest in Toe couldn't help but grow as my interest in the gospel grew, and during the hours we spent on the phone during those weeks we often shared personal ideas and dreams, dislikes and likes, goals and desires. A fast friendship developed, though I would have liked for it to have been more than just friendship. We even talked about marriage—not for us, but about the principle in general. And one night as we talked about eternal marriage and its relationship to the priesthood Toe told me—in answer to my direct question—that she would never be able to marry a black man because he couldn't take her to the temple and they couldn't have their children sealed to them forever. A knot formed in my heart and pangs of confusion swept through me.

The whole idea of eternal marriage sounded great to me. But it didn't seem fair that I should be automatically disqualified from something that I had no control over. I'm sure that this is when the whole concept of eternal marriage really started becoming important to me: the principle hit a little too close to home because it threatened the relationship that I hoped would eventually develop between Toe and me.

"What difference does the priesthood really make? Every man can be a minister," I finally said one evening.

Toe tried her best to explain that because the priesthood is the power to act for God here on this earth, it is the foundation of family and Church life.

"We don't completely know why your people can't hold the priesthood," she concluded. Once again a pain seared through my heart. Even though we'd only talked on the phone, I felt that the Lord had a special reason for bringing us together—and I told Toe how I felt. I even thought—and hoped—that she would be my wife one day.

But as the days went by and I continued to grow more confused about the whole situation, I finally decided that I might as well quit being frustrated and disappointed. Instead, I determined to be happy just knowing Toe and having contact with her.

Though I tried to improve my attitude about my relationship with Toe, the day came when I had had enough of these talks over the phone. After all, I hadn't even seen Toe since that first time at the Cultural Center. Yet we'd developed a relationship by talking for hours over the phone over a period of two weeks. I felt like I knew her much better than I really did. So with all the charisma and irresistible charm I could muster, I called her one evening and somehow persuaded her to go out on a date with me.

With her final words—"Well, yes, but I just want you to know that I could never marry a Negro"—ringing in my ears, I drove over to get her that night. And you know, at that point I almost didn't care. I just wanted to see again this girl who had become so much a part of my life.

For some reason I expected to see waiting for me a Polynesian girl, sitting on a mat, dressed in her native costume when I pulled up at Toe's dorm. So as I walked toward the dorm I passed right by her—until, that is, she touched me on the arm and asked, "Hi, Brother Freeman"—she was already calling me that—"are you ready to go?"

I did a double-take. No, she definitely was *not* that brown-skinned little native girl that I had seen several weeks earlier sitting on the mat. This young woman was dressed in a pantsuit, and her hair was different, and, well, she was just beautiful! I silently congratulated myself once again on what fine taste I had, and I led her to the car.

I couldn't for the life of me tell you what movie we saw that night. My mind was on other things. As we walked out of the movie my excitement at being with Toe finally got the best of me, and I picked her up and swung her around and around in the air. I'm sure she wondered what kind of mad man she'd consented to go out with, but I was so thrilled to be with her that nothing could have bothered me.

Later that evening I found out a little more about this intriguing girl. We stopped for something to eat and I offered her a Coke. Well, that launched a little discussion on the Word of Wisdom—which was, incidentally, the first time I'd been introduced to that doctrine. From the Word of Wisdom our conversation progressed to include other principles of the gospel and, as it had when we talked on the phone, time slipped away as Toe shared with me these truths she held so sacred.

Hearing Toe's words about the gospel over the phone was one thing; but being with her and feeling of her spirit and conviction was entirely another. That evening I felt myself drawn like a magnet to both the gospel and Toe. I knew that I must do something about my growing knowledge, interest, and belief in this church; and I felt just as certain that I wanted to do something about my relationship with Toe. There was something so sweet and special about her that words can't even begin to describe the feelings that flooded my heart that night. I was overwhelmed by the emotion that surged through me. Now, of course, I can see that it was the combination of my attraction to Toe and the gospel which touched my heart so deeply.

Time finally proved the victor, and I had to say goodnight. I leaned over and gave her a little kiss as I left her at her door. (I think she was surprised that I didn't bite her. She told me later that one of her friends once told her that black people eat one another.) With that kiss I floated home, wondering how I would convince her to see me again and also wondering how I would resolve these many mixed feelings I had about the gospel.

Toe helped me with the second dilemma, because she lost no time in resuming her missionary work with me. She had two girlfriends, Polili and Kinamoni, whom I'd become acquainted with, and Polili had aready set up a missionary appointment for two friends of hers from the Baha'i faith. Toe asked me to come and meet these missionaries, which I was glad to do.

I considered the opportunity of meeting with the missionaries to be a special one, because I, as a minister, would be meeting two missionaries who were also ministers. So out of respect for their positions in the Mormon Church I put on my best suit and tie.

Because of the other investigators, the meeting turned out to be very interesting. Without really giving the missionaries a chance to present their discussion, the investigators began an incessant stream of questions, dwelling particularly on the Negro/priesthood issue. Nothing the missionaries could say would satisfy the two men. I thought it a little amusing that I, being the only black present, was less agitated by the whole question of the Negroes and the priesthood than the white men were. I wasn't very impressed or interested at all as I listened to the argument that ensued over this issue; even though the missionaries tried to stay away from an argument, the two men persisted.

While the doctrinal discussion was going on, my mind drifted to many things. I think that for the first time I really asked myself if this church could possibly be true. And if it was, I asked myself, what was I going to do about it? I'd always said that I was a seeker of truth and light and that I wanted to do anything that would bring me closer to Jesus Christ. Yes, I'd always *said* these things. But now my whole heritage and the things I'd believed for as long as I could remember were in jeopardy.

What if this church were really true? Could I admit it to myself? Could I actually join a church where I would not be eligible—and might never be—to hold the priesthood, to be a minister? Could I give up the ministry that I had worked so hard to obtain, that meant so much to me? How could it be possible for me to give up doing what I loved most?

These thoughts seared my heart and plagued my mind as I drove home that night. My life had changed so quickly, it seemed. Six weeks ago I had never heard of Toe Isapela Leituala and I had known little or nothing about the gospel. And now, heavy questions and potential changes clouded my thoughts and my future.

The missionaries had challenged me to read the Book of Mormon and to heed Moroni's counsel and accept the challenge to find out if the book is true. For if the Book of Mormon is truly the word of God, then it stands to reason that the other principles of Mormonism are true as well. And I already knew that. I already felt quite sure that the concepts I'd been taught in the past weeks were those of truth and light. I felt that there was every possibility that this church was led by him whose church it was, Jesus the Christ.

I got home a little after 10:00 P.M. and began immediately to read. And I don't believe I got past even the first verse in Nephi, for when I read the words, "I, Nephi, having been born of goodly parents, therefore I was taught somewhat in the learning of my father," my mind went back to those questions that had haunted me during the meeting with the missionaries. I thought of my goodly parents. How I loved them! How I appreciated the love and direction they had always given me! I remembered the family prayers we held together and the times we sang gospel hymns around the piano; the many evenings when choir practice was held in our home; the countless mornings I'd been so proud of my mother as she spoke from the pulpit, calling people to repentance and challenging them to walk uprightly before the Lord. Those scenes flashed before my mind so realistically and so quickly that I could barely keep my eyes open because of the tears that rolled down my face. I searched my soul; was I going to leave these things that I had known all my life? Was I going to turn my back on everything that had meant so much to me?

My mother had always cautioned me to not be as a boat without a sail and a rudder, a boat which goes any way the wind blows. But she also said that if I would always search the scriptures that I could always find my course from them—they would never lead me astray. I had tried to do that all of my life. And now because of it, I was being torn in halves—my spirit was already responding to the true gospel, but my heart was with my family, with the church that was so familiar, with my burning desire to preach the gospel and to help others.

Yet I could sense that I was in the process of finding in the Mormon Church that security and feeling that I'd felt missing as I'd preached in the Holiness Church. Because of that I forced these heartwrenching images out of my mind and returned my eyes to the page. As I read about Lehi and the struggles he went through as he convinced his family that they should leave their home in Jerusalem and journey into the wilderness, I thought that maybe I would have to "leave" my parents—for a while, that is—to seek out the truth. And the more I read the better I began to feel, for the words became very sweet to me. Peace and a certain calm eased the pain in my heart. I read late into the night as the words of Nephi, then Jacob, and even later, King Benjamin, soothed my soul. I think I knew that the time was soon approaching when I would know for sure, one way or the other, if this gospel was all I supposed it might be.

The next few days were filled with reading the Book of Mormon. Not only did my soul respond to what it contained, but the logic of such a book stood out like a sore thumb to me. I had always wondered what the scripture in Revelation about an angel bringing more knowledge to the earth meant. I had never been given an explanation before that had satisfied me. And I had always personally believed that Christ must have visited people other than the Jews, because he always talked about the "sheep I have which are not of this fold."

It seemed very logical to me that a record would be made of and by those people, just as the Bible was the history of the Jews. The Book of Mormon concept of the peopling of the American continent was more feasible than any I'd ever heard. I'd never been able to accept other explanations or theories concerning many of the ambiguous doctrines. Now everything seemed to fit together in my mind like a giant jigsaw puzzle.

Yet I knew that logic was only one facet of a testimony of the gospel; my spirit would have to be touched by the Spirit in order for me to know that this was in fact the gospel of Jesus Christ.

During the following days I spent many more hours on the phone with Toe, asking questions about the gospel and always growing with the insight she had to share with me. I stood in awe of her knowledge and understanding of the scriptures; her understanding went beyond my own, and I was even an ordained minister! But she told me things that were mind-boggling. She explained some of the biblical scriptures that had always been a mystery to me (such as the ones referring to Joseph Smith and the verse about the small rock beginning to roll until it became a great boulder.)

Toe told me that I was a man searching for happiness, and that if I'd only allow it, I could find happiness in the gospel. She emphasized that I had a mission in this life and a future to look forward to; she taught me that I was created in the likeness of God, both physically and spiritually, and that the Lord wanted me to develop a spiritual relationship with him in this life that would extend to eternity. And when she told me that the gospel was the center of her life and that she loved it with all her heart, I knew that she was sincere.

The weekend following my visit with the missionaries I had a unique experience. Toe and the other local Church members were all excited about a quarterly conference that was to be held at the Cultural Center. The Regional Representative and some General Authorities were going to be there. Although I didn't completely understand the significance of those officials, I was sure they were very important in the Church organization.

I turned out to be as impressed with this conference as everyone had told me I'd be. Two choirs—one Samoan and one Tongan—provided the music, and it was absolutely magnificent. I was greatly impressed by these islanders who provided such beautiful music a cappella. I enjoyed the speakers, too; their messages were all well thought-out and impressively delivered. I felt almost like I was back home when the stake president began his talk. He pounded on the pulpit and preached "fire and brimstone" doctrine, sort of like an old Baptist or Holiness preacher would.

But even in a congregation as large as this one I didn't go unnoticed. Kinamoni, who was sitting by Toe and me, was picked at random by the Regional Representative during his talk and asked to stand up.

"What are you doing to help bring the gospel to the people of Hawaii, young lady?" he asked.

Kinamoni was short, only about 4'10'', and shy, but she was brave when it came to the gospel. She replied, "Well, I happen to be sitting by a young black minister whom we took to the missionaries this very week."

With that, I could just feel what was coming next. The Regional Representative looked at me and asked me to stand and introduce myself, which I did. This was actually sort of an honor to me, as I felt that I was being recognized (and honored) as a minister visiting from another faith. Who would ever have thought that in my first Mormon conference I'd be standing to introduce myself to the crowd? All the way around there was nothing "normal" about my introduction to the gospel, and this conference proved no different.

After the conference I felt I ought to start attending church regularly, but that was a big and rather awkward step to take and I wasn't quite sure how to go about it. Again this was remedied very easily. I happened to be talking to our inactive Mormon sergeant one afternoon and mentioned to him that I was interested in the Church. Before I could blink he'd pulled out a phone book and was running his finger down the page, looking for the bishop of the nearest ward. He made contact with the bishop, and the following Sunday missionaries were waiting at the door as both the sergeant and I walked up the front steps.

After that first meeting, I began attending church meetings regularly, especially fast and testimony meetings. The first afternoon that I sat in a testimony meeting, I found myself amazed with what took place. Many bore testimony of the truthfulness of the gospel, as we did in the Holiness Church. I was particularly touched as two young people, with tears streaming down their cheeks, stood to share their feelings. Their tears ran down their cheeks and into my heart as I felt the spirit of what they said and also as I reflected back to earlier days when, as a young man, I had stood to bear my testimony of Jesus Christ in a similar manner.

After this experience, the light in my room was frequently on into the wee hours of the morning as I read and studied the Book of Mormon. I spent hours on my knees, often fasting as well. I felt drawn to Enos, for my soul hungered to know, to feel with a burning that this gospel was true. I felt an urgency to know that Joseph Smith was truly a prophet of God—that through him had been restored to this earth that which had been taken so very long ago—because in almost every other area of doctrine I felt drawn to this gospel. The plan of salvation dealing with the premortal life and the three degrees of glory was sensible to me. As a member of the Holiness Church it had been difficult for me to visualize what type of judgment or reward we were working for. Ideas about angels, white robes, clouds, and a life without pain were some of the attributes we supposed heaven contained. But to know that we have the potential of godhood if we live righteously and fulfill the measure of our creation by sharing the mansions on high with our Elder Brother—that was a concept full of light, motivation, and truth.

The belief that Adam was not responsible for all the world's transgressions appealed to me. I had never felt comfortable and justified in saddling Adam with the world's problems, but felt him instead to be one of the greatest men who have ever lived; after all, he and Eve are our parents.

Temple marriage, although it appeared to be something that I couldn't participate in, was the most beautiful concept of marriage I had ever heard. I truly believed that the father should function as a patriarch in his own home; that parents should remain loyal and faithful to themselves and to their children; and that the family unit was the basis of all civilization. So to think that couples who lived worthily could be sealed together, with their children, forever was an amazingly simple yet overwhelming thought.

This church was organized as Christ had organized his church in the meridian of time. Hadn't I always sought this very thing? Hadn't I had a nagging feeling that there might be a church patterned after Christ's primitive church?

Baptism for the dead, the law of tithing, Sabbath-day observance, the Word of Wisdom, the concepts of premortal and postmortal life, and the overall spirit that the people themselves seemed to carry with them all were directly in line with beliefs I'd already had or which had come to seem very logical and natural to me. But there were only two things which still bothered me—two things which stood in the way of the Spirit manifesting to me the truthfulness of the gospel: I needed to know that Joseph Smith was a true prophet; and it disturbed me that there were no other (or very few) black faces in Mormon congregations.

The members of my family were all good people concerned with living the Holiness gospel as best they could. How was it that I was the only one to have found this new religion? And how was it that other members of my own race had not been drawn to this church if it was the true church? I felt that I could finally jump the hurdle of not being allowed to hold the priesthood if I truly knew the Church to be true—even though it would mean an end to my own preaching of the gospel.

I had great faith in a just and fair God. And even though many told me that I might be able to hold the priesthood in the next life, I felt sure that somehow I *would* hold the priesthood. I was concerned about being denied the blessings of temple marriage, but at this point in time I had the misconception that this ordinance could be performed in my behalf after I died. I knew that God was not a respecter of persons, and that if I lived worthily things would somehow turn out okay.

So I wasn't particularly threatened nor did I really feel discriminated against because of the Negro/priesthood policy. But I couldn't understand why I was the only black in Hawaii (or at least I had seen no others) to be drawn to the Church. And in North Carolina I had grown up without ever even hearing of the Church! Weren't there any Mormons in North Carolina? It just seemed unbelievable to think I had to come nearly five thousand miles to find the truth.

But as I thought about these things I had to catch myself: I had truly been seeking these past months for something better, something that would give me the added depth of spirituality and power I felt I needed. I'd spent hours on my knees, even before ever visiting the Polynesian Cultural Center, asking the Lord that I might find my wife—a woman who would support me in my ministerial role. Had the Lord answered my prayers now by diverting my steps from American Samoa where I had almost spent my military leave to the Cultural Center, where I had been introduced to Mormonism and Toe? I had to find out, and I knew that the only thing which stood between me and being baptized into the Church was a testimony that Joseph Smith was a prophet.

The next few days found me either on my knees, on the phone talking to Toe, or reading the Book of Mormon. And as I read I gradually began to have confirmed in my heart what I suspected. I did "ask with a sincere heart, with real intent, having faith in Christ" whether the Book of Mormon was true. And though even to this day I can't pinpoint a specific moment, the Holy Ghost did manifest the truth of it to me.

From that manifestation came an overwhelming burning within me that Joseph Smith was a prophet of God; that he had been chosen to be the instrument in the hands of the Lord whereby the gospel was restored to the earth. I knew the gospel was true! I knew that I had to become a member of it. Though giving up my ministryship would no doubt fill me with a certain loneliness and void, I couldn't imagine the emptiness and inner turmoil that would come from ignoring what I knew to be true—especially when I had been pleading with the Lord for so long to show me what it was that I knew I was lacking.

Who would have ever believed that I, Joseph Freeman, Jr., a small-town boy from North Carolina who had been reared in the Holiness faith, and who was even an ordained minister of that faith, would travel all the way to the Hawaiian Islands, come in contact with the Mormons (an almost all-white church), step down from my ministryship, and be baptized into a church that I had not even known about a few months earlier? It does sound nearly impossible, yet the Lord does move in mysterious ways. Yes, I knew that I would soon take one of the biggest steps of my life by becoming a member of The Church of Jesus Christ of Latter-day Saints.

By the time the next fast and testimony meeting rolled around, I stood to bear my testimony other members of the Church, for I, too, was a member, having entered the waters of baptism on September 30, 1973.

Love and Marriage

I could tell the difference. Though my lifestyle didn't change all that drastically, the quality of my life improved. And with each day the gift of the Holy Ghost became a greater source of guidance and peace and a more permanent part of my life. It wasn't long before I echoed those words we often hear in testimony meeting: "I don't know how I ever lived without the gospel."

Joining the Church brought with it a lot of challenges, though—perhaps the greatest being that it was sometimes easy to feel like a duck out of water. I felt relatively alone when it came to sharing the gospel with my own friends, with people of my own race. No more Shadrach, Meshach, and Abednego. No more three-day fasts, ending up in the Holiness Church to pray with good friends. And there's definitely something intimidating about being the only black man to walk into a chapel full of white people. Of course, this particular situation was alleviated somewhat just by being in Hawaii—a land where even white skin tends to be brown. And Hawaii is a great "fruit basket" of nationalities anyway. So often I'd find myself sitting between one member from Japan and another from Taiwan, or

Samoa, or even a native Hawaiian. And after a while, these faces became people and the people became friends. It's amazing what a little love can do to jump the race (or any other) barrier.

Time passed, and I jumped headlong into studying even more diligently about the doctrines and practices of this new church. As you might expect, I was especially concerned about the Negro/priesthood question. For the first six months I read everything I could get my hands on that dealt in even a remote way with this subject. Though I had felt good about joining a church that had restrictions placed upon members of my race, and though I had dealt with any qualms I had about the whole situation before I was baptized, as my knowledge and love of the gospel increased it became important for me to understand the reasons behind the priesthood restriction; it became crucial that I justify it in my mind so that, when the day came, I could justify it to my children in such a way that they wouldn't resent the Church. After all, I was being penalized for something that, for at least the time being, I had no control over.

Of course there were many theories on this topic, and I read and listened to and analyzed them all. Some said Negroes were the unvaliant ones in the pre-earth life. Others said we were the fence-sitters who couldn't decide whether to follow Christ or Satan. Some said that our hearts leaned to the side of Satan even though we made the choice to follow Christ.

All of this was rather disturbing because I couldn't find scriptural proof for any of it. Finally, after much study and prayer it dawned on me that we did not really know why this limitation had been placed on my race; no prophet had ever explained the exact reason. The important thing—the foundation to anchor myself to—was that I knew Joseph Smith was a prophet and that the Book of Mormon was the word of God; and more importantly, I knew for sure that this was Christ's church. I certainly knew that God loved me, that he cared about me individually, and that he was a just God.

Suddenly I didn't worry anymore, for I felt certain that the time would come—whether it be in the Millennium as most people said, or even in this life—when I would be able to hold the priesthood. Holding the priesthood didn't seem such an impossible dream, because my concept of the Millennium was not of some faraway thing that was beyond comprehension; I really felt that it might not be very many years before that "great and dreadful day"—maybe it would even arrive in my lifetime. If it did arrive during my lifetime, well, I could surely wait that long. My challenge was to be worthy whenever the call would come.

Yes, things were going well for me. Pretty well, that is, with one major exception: Toe. I hadn't seen her since the day I had been baptized, and we'd only talked a time or two on the phone. After that first date, I had charmed her into going out with me on a few more "real" dates. In addition, we spent time together with the missionaries and then talked often on the phone, so our friendship did grow. From my point of view there was certainly the potential of more than just a friendship. But Toe—or Isa, as I had begun calling her, since Isapela was her middle name—really hesitated to see me very often. Somehow she had the notion firmly planted in her mind that if we dated very much, we'd end up getting married. There was no way she was going to allow that to happen. She had made it very clear (in a nice way, of course) that she just could not risk falling in love with a black man. That was a dead-end road as far as she was concerned.

I had even taken a night security job at the Cultural Center, hoping I would see Toe more often that way. I'd frequently cook her dinner and take it to her. I thought maybe in this case the way to a *woman's* heart would be through her stomach. But my whole effort wasn't very successful because Toe was called to be the Relief Society president in her student branch at the Church College of Hawaii, and needless to say, that calling demanded most of her time. Because it became so apparent that Toe was increasingly nervous and hesitant about building a relationship with me, we finally both decided to decrease the amount of time we spent together and even the time we talked on the phone; I think we could both tell that our feelings were starting to get involved. If this relationship wasn't going to go anywhere, maybe "getting out while the getting's good" was the best policy. So after I was baptized, our contact, even as friends, suddenly and sharply almost ceased.

I wasn't very happy about the whole situation, but I didn't see that there was much I could do to change things. After all, life does go on. Mine did, anyway, and since I'm a loner by nature (I've always said that Me, Myself, and I hang pretty close together) I managed to survive. But the Church has a way of infiltrating every corner of your life, and it wasn't long before I'd formed some fast friendships.

Polili Alofepo, one of the girls that had been with Isa and me in that first meeting with the missionaries, lived with her family across the island. She and the members of her family struck up a relationship with me that soon blossomed into one of those rare and special relationships that come so seldom in a lifetime. It wasn't long before I could be found, at least one day every week, over at Polili's house. I would fill a bag with groceries, hop on the bus, and head to my "second family's" house to make a day of it.

As happens when you spend time, feelings, and experiences together, the Alofepos and I became very close, and one of the fringe benefits of loyal friends is that they're bound to speak highly of you. Well, these family members turned out to be great public relations agents, and whenever they mentioned me to others it was always in a very complimentary way. Though I didn't realize it at the time, they were to prove to be my greatest asset at a most crucial time.

You see, Isapela was also a very close friend of the Alofepos. But I didn't know that. In fact, unbeknown to me, Isa and Polili were like sisters, and, of course, they confided in each other as sisters (and girls) always do. Well, Polili fancied herself the matchmaker to end all matchmakers, and she had decided that Isa and I "were just made for each other." Why we couldn't seem to get together was beyond her understanding. She was just sure, though, that any little obstacles keeping us apart could be overcome, and she therefore assigned herself to take on the whole matter as her personal project.

She began by working on Toe, telling her all the reasons we would be just perfect together. What's more, Polili had the amazing ability to convince anyone of almost anything; and it wasn't long before Toe was thinking that maybe she'd been a little hasty in her decision to end our growing friendship. As I say, Polili can do my public relations work anytime. After hearing her sales pitch on me, I think she could sell sand to a desert nomad.

Well, the day came when I became the object of the matchmaker's plot. Early in November during one of my weekly visits to Polili's house, Polili seemed unusually anxious to have my undivided attention. She monopolized my time, finding millions of things for us to do, and as the day wore on she gradually initiated a conversation that soon focused on Toe. Before I knew it we were talking about Toe and me and the possibilities of our dating again. Of course, she weaseled out of me some of my thoughts about the whole situation in general and about Toe in particular, and I tried to explain gently to her that Toe had let me know in no uncertain terms that we had no future together. I, for one, just couldn't see the point of belaboring something that was a closed issue and was very sensitive as well. But when she made sure that I still had very strong feelings for Toe, Polili sprang it on me: "Toe wants to see you again."

I couldn't imagine why on earth Toe had changed her mind—the color of my skin was still black, and I still couldn't hold the priesthood. Naturally, though, I told Polili that I'd be glad to see Isa again; and as I got up to leave I mentioned that I'd give her a call in a day or two.

"Oh, you don't have to do that," was Polili's reply. My puzzled look turned into one of incredulity as Toe walked through the adjoining door. She had been in the next room the whole time! Did I feel stupid! No one can tell me that women don't have a little bit of natural conniving in them!

After I recovered from the mild shock, Isa walked me out to the car; and, true to Polili's words, she said, "When can we get together? Let's do it soon."

I just happened to have the perfect occasion. My sergeant had phoned me just a day or two earlier with an invitation for Toe and me (he didn't realize that we hadn't dated for quite a while) to join him for Thanksgiving dinner. So I asked if she'd do me the honor of being my companion for Thanksgiving dinner, and she seemed delighted to accept. (She was not half as delighted as I was, of course.)

So on Thanksgiving Day, almost two months since we'd been together, Isapela and I had one of the few real dates we'd had since first meeting each other; and it was one of only four or five occasions we'd been together that hadn't been missionary-oriented. I decided beforehand that I'd better make the most of this date. Who knew how long this changed attitude of Toe's would last?

I picked Isa up—she looked sensational! It was hard for me to even be objective at this point about the girl who had helped me find the gospel—a woman whose ideals far surpassed even my own expectations. I'd planned things so that we had time alone together both before and after the dinner. There's no doubt about it—I was ready to give this date my "best shot" romantically.

We drove out to a beach at Waianae—the perfect place to charm a girl, I thought. We talked and just enjoyed being together. The dinner at the sergeant's house followed, and things there couldn't have been more perfect if I'd planned them myself. The small details became so important—sitting together at the table, joking with each other, being at ease in a social situation, enjoying a stolen glance or two as our eyes met. I don't want to sound mushy or anything, but as all who've fallen in love know, there's nothing quite as exciting as trying to win the heart of the girl you love. Even the smallest details become critical; each wink or glance or toss of her head steals just a little bit more of your heart.

As Toe and I said our thank you's and good-byes and walked to the car, I thought that the day could not have been more perfect. But the best was yet to come.

On the drive home we stopped at a small park on a beach to just relax. We ran through the sand, swung in the swings, laughed, and talked—just as the couples do in all the pictures on the Hallmark greetings cards. As we sat on the grass, talking and getting to know each other better, I could sense that a change had come over Toe. I didn't feel her pulling away from me; I no longer had the frustrating sensation that I needed to hold on because this was the last time I'd see her. Something had changed, and as we talked and laughed and joked I was sure I could sense that change.

We had been laughing and teasing each other and suddenly, without warning and in an almost flippant way, she looked me straight in the eye and said, "Well, when do you want to get married?"

I'm sure I looked as though I'd fainted, or at least seen a ghost. Then I realized she was partly joking. I was stunned, because I knew that her anxieties and concerns about falling in love with me must have been at least partially resolved in her mind. She was actually considering the possibility of marrying me! Unbelievable! I felt like I had the world by the tail! I was—I mean, *we* were—in love!

From that point on we entered the difficult period of time when we had to decide if we were *supposed* to marry each other. It seemed that there was so much against it from the start. We knew that we'd fallen in love with each other; we both felt we'd found someone whose commitment to righteous principles was what we wanted in a marriage partner. But was it *right*?

Let me say here that, even though in the end we did marry, that does not mean that I could advise someone else to make an interracial marriage. Our leaders have warned us about the dangers involved. President Kimball has said, ''Experience of the Brethren through a hundred years has proved to us that marriage is a very difficult thing under any circumstances, and the difficulty increases in interrace marriages.'' And again, ''We recommend that people marry those who are of the same racial background generally.'' In this crucial matter the two people concerned would need to be very sure they had the Lord's approval before embarking on such a marriage.

It's tricky enough for anyone—and especially a member of the Church—to make this once-in-a-lifetime decision. Your whole eternal welfare is at stake. Happiness and personal welfare here on earth are only the beginning, because what we all desire is the great joy that is possible for couples who live worthy of having their marriage sealed by the Holy Spirit of Promise.

But the consequences are much more complicated when a man and woman enter into an interracial marriage. We knew this. To add just one more log to the fire, we were from completely different backgrounds and cultures. My boyhood on the farm in North Carolina couldn't have been more different than Toe's growing-up years on an island in Samoa. On paper it looked rather silly that we should even consider marrying each other, but our hearts told us there must be a way.

I was black; she was brown. I was American; she was Samoan; and there is an almost natural antagonism between Negroes and Polynesians. She had been through the temple; it seemed unlikely that I could ever do that. The men did the cooking in Samoa; I expected my wife to take care of that. Toe wanted to return to Samoa to live; I was a North Carolina farm boy, and I always supposed that's where I'd end up. Toe's patriarchal blessing said that her husband "will be known in the gates when he is seated among the elders of the land"; she didn't see how that could be referring to me.

But as overwhelming as these obstacles and differences were, we shared some things in common. We both had been reared in religious, non-LDS homes and were converts to the gospel; we both knew the gospel to be true and desired to pattern our home around it; we both had come from large families (Toe had thirteen brothers and sisters) and we both wanted to have a large family of our own; all my life I'd wanted to be a minister, and Toe's stepfather (who was a London Missionary Society minister) had always wanted her to marry a minister; I had felt from the start that something special had drawn Toe and me together—something even more than the gospel—and she finally admitted that she had felt that way, too; we had the same goals, desires, and dreams of this life; and to top it all off, we really loved each other.

For days we debated the pros and cons of our prospective marriage—and this isn't a particularly easy thing to do objectively when emotions are so involved. As you might imagine, we had many advisers—everyone thought they knew what was best for us. And really, they were only trying to help and show their concern. But with only a couple of exceptions (Polili and her family being the main ones), few shared the enthusiasm about our possible marriage that our matchmaker did.

Other mutual friends, Toe's teachers and associates at school, and members of the Church felt very strongly that we should not marry—and didn't hesitate to give us that advice. As a matter of fact, some were very insistent about it. I was black and Toe was not. It was open and shut. There was no way we were meant to be together.

In theory I could understand their concerns, yet my heart told me differently. I felt so good about marrying Toe, and I didn't view our marriage as something that would be harmful or condescending to Toe. She gained a peaceful and calm feeling about our marriage, too. What these self-appointed counselors and advisers didn't realize was that we were both very earnest in seeking the Lord through fasting and prayer because, though we both sincerely desired this marriage to be his will, neither of us was willing to go through with it without divine approval and confirmation.

After receiving a barrage of negative opinions and feelings, we felt the need for counsel from our priesthood authorities, and we took the problem to our stake president. We told him that we had definite concerns about entering an interracial and intercultural marriage, and that many had counseled us against forming this union; that we had fasted and prayed about marriage; that we loved each other; but that we wanted most of all to do what was right for us and what was pleasing to the Lord. He listened to all of this patiently and sensitively; when we finished he began to speak and, believe me, we listened.

He counseled us about the challenges and great responsibilities that naturally come with any marriage, as I'm sure he counseled all couples who were considering this big step. But he didn't stop there. Very honestly and forthrightly he explained the built-in additional difficulties that accompany an intercultural marriage, and he particularly emphasized the awkward position Toe would be in if she married me, a man who could not give her the security of a marriage sealed for eternity in the house of the Lord nor who could bless her home with the priesthood. But when he finished with this counsel he told us he felt impressed to say that if we would both fast and pray about this decision, we would know if the Lord approved our marriage. If we then felt this to be the case, he said, we should go ahead and be married. He assured us that if we did feel confirmation from the Lord that we would be blessed in our marriage and we would be able to overcome the problems that would arise.

We did just as he advised us. After much fasting and prayer, both together and individually, we both felt that the Lord did approve of our marriage. I don't think that either she or I was looking through rose-colored glasses; we knew that the road ahead would not be the easiest and that we would both have to be flexible, understanding, giving, loving, and sacrificing. But then, don't all newly married couples face the same challenges as they learn to live and grow together?

We set the date—June 15, 1974. I was ecstatic! I was marrying the kind of girl I'd always dreamed of, and I felt my parents would be happy about my choice. And they were.

Most engaged couples go through several stages during their engagement that tempt them to call off the wedding. One is the cold-feet syndrome; another is the "Have I made the right choice?" dilemma. Neither of these really affected Toe or me; but even after we'd made the decision to marry there were many who continued to try to persuade us to call it off. After hearing this as often as I did, I began to wonder if I was cheating Toe out of the kind of man she deserved. I wondered if she'd be ashamed of me after we married—embarrassed that I was her husband. After all, I couldn't even bless our children. And it wasn't as though she had never been to the temple herself; she had experienced the joy of increased knowledge and understanding that comes through attending the temple, and I couldn't participate with her in that. Maybe I was taking advantage of her because I loved her so much.

Each day found me more depressed about this, and of course this didn't help Toe's spirits, either, so I went with a heavy heart to talk to my bishop. This wasn't my first trip to see him, and he knew full well the situation at hand. He listened to my worries and then counseled me by saying, "I can understand how you must feel. But you've both felt confident about the Lord's will in your situation. And the Lord doesn't change his mind. But because you're so concerned about Toe's well-being, and if you really love Toe and she really loves you, then it's up to her to make this decision. Give her the privilege of answering this question. Don't you decide for her in advance that you are hurting her and that you won't be the quality husband she deserves."

Now as I look back I'm sure this whole question plagued me much more than it did Toe. I really went through some rough days, though, because I loved her enough that I didn't want to deprive her of the blessings she deserved. And I certainly didn't want to be an embarrassment to her after we were married. How damaging that could be to both her and my self-esteem!

After all this worry, though, when I did finally sit down and talk with Toe about it, she looked at me in amazement that I would even suggest not getting married. She had made up her mind, and she felt calm and secure about it.

After this little trauma, I thought it would be clear skies ahead until the big day. But Toe had her "moment of truth" as well. I was at work one day when the phone rang, and instead of the usually cheerful Toe on the line I was surprised to hear her shaking and crying voice.

"Joseph, I just don't feel like we'd better get married. I don't know what it is, but I'm really scared and think this just might be too big a step for me. Please don't make me say any more, because I love you too much and I can't bear to hurt you any more than I already have. Good-bye, Joe."

I thought my heart would burst. I couldn't stand the thought that I had lost my dear bride-to-be. And I couldn't understand it. We had already withstood the storm of making the decisions; we'd overcome the opinions of others; we had both felt confident that the Lord sanctioned our marriage. Why this?

Yet, if Toe didn't feel good about things, I didn't want to marry her. I wasn't going to talk her into something she didn't eagerly desire herself. So I decided to let her go.

But that night when I fell to my knees in prayer, weary from the emotional strain of the day, I sought from our Heavenly Father a reassurance that Toe's decision was his will. I had to have something to ease my pain—something to hang on to. The longer I prayed the more I felt that we were still meant to be together. So I did the only thing I could do—I left my faith and prayers in the hands of the Lord by asking him that if he saw fit that Toe and I should be together that he would provide a way for us to become husband and wife. And I promised in return that I would do everything in my power to love her and our children and to teach them the things of righteousness all of the days of our lives. I promised that our family would do all we could to be instruments in his hands, to be used as he saw fit. With that prayer and covenant embedded in my heart, I rose from my knees, confident that the Lord would provide a way if it was his will.

The very next day the phone rang again. Still in a shaky voice, Toe asked if we could get together and talk about things. We did, and she confided in me her fears about our marriage; but she also said that she'd felt miserable all night and had asked the Lord for guidance. She felt sure that she should marry me, though her worries were not entirely gone.

As we talked and prayed together that evening, the Lord blessed us with a peaceful reassurance of our relationship, and we each knew that we were ready to take upon ourselves the responsibility of creating a happy, productive, fulfilling marriage. And we knew the Lord was on our side.

This proved to be our last big hurdle before the wedding. Finally, on June 15, 1974, we were married in the Hauula Second Ward by Bishop Joseph Ah Quin, better known in Hawaii as the "Singing Bishop." And with that I realized my dream of marrying a girl fit to be a minister's wife—a woman who would live the gospel and love the Lord with all her heart.

A Wife Lost
and Found

There is a certain sense of peace and righteousness (and certainly great happiness) that comes with living with the right woman. Marriage to Toe was (and is) a little piece of heaven. Things couldn't have started out better. Here I was, married to Toe, and, unlike many who choose the romantic island of Hawaii to spend their honeymoon, Toe and I had our beautiful surroundings to enjoy even beyond the first week or ten days of our marriage. Truly I felt like my whole world was a little paradise of its own.

How my life had changed in the past year! I was married to the beautiful Samoan girl who had introduced me to the other great treasure in my life—the gospel. I had satisfied and calmed an inner turmoil that had raged within me for years by finding and accepting the light and truth of the gospel. The Lord had really blessed me.

As Toe and I began our life together we found the words of our stake president to be very true. There was much for us to learn about sharing, giving, adapting, and loving. We weren't married for very long before we found out what all young married people quickly discover—that their partner is not perfect. Not yet, at least. But aside from how I rolled the toothpaste tube and my habit of throwing soiled socks under the bed, we began to discover other more important things about each other—those types of things that come to light as you live and grow together.

And of course we had an added area of discovery that quickly became obvious in our life together—our completely different backgrounds. Toe's growing-up years were so different from my own; and yet, as opposite as our growing-up years and experiences were, we found an amazing number of similarities as well. Each new day became an exciting adventure which promised additional discoveries.

Toe came from a large family, being one of fourteen children. When she had been fifteen, her father had passed away; consequently, the children were divided among relatives and close friends to be reared. Toe found her way into the home of good friends of the family who were members of the London Missionary Society, her stepfather being a minister in that church. Because of this her life was one that centered around religion, as mine had been with my minister mother.

The lifestyle in Samoa is so different from that in the United States that it was hard for me to imagine. Toe grew up eating bread-fruit, yams, taro, oo from the coconut, chocolate from cocoa beans, and, best of all, palusami made from taro leaves and coconut milk. A day without a swim in the ocean was unheard of, as everyone had to swim. There is no such thing as rent or light bills on the island of Samoa, and each family owns the land their home is on. The food is prepared in a large, open, outdoor pit called an umu, and by tradition the men prepare the main portion of the meals.

Samoan life is governed by island chiefs, and each family has a family chief who represents his family at the village meetings. The family chief makes the basic decisions for the family unit—a unit that includes brothers and sisters, their mates and children, and the children's companions. He might, for example, decide which part of their land will be farmed and where family houses will be built. He calls the family together to decide who will represent the family as the future family chief—a man who must have a high character and other leadership qualities.

The Samoan people are very giving and generous; everything is shared between family members—food, clothing, and money. In fact, if a family knows of another family that is without food, it is only right and is even expected of them to prepare a basket of food along with their own meal and take it over to the other family even before they themselves eat.

Likewise, if you go into another's home in Samoa and notice something you especially like—such as a picture on the wall or a beautifully woven mat—the owner will oftentimes give the object to you, even if it's a prized possession. In this way, Toe's and my backgrounds were very similar, as my parents have always lived by the "What Is Ours Is Yours" motto.

Each Samoan family awakens its members and begins the day together with a song and prayer. Again in the evening at around seven the bells ring and everyone should, by that time, already be gathered in their homes for song and prayer. This custom is not voluntary— anyone who is found on the streets during these times is automatically fined. No one is allowed to walk out of the house for any reason during this time. On Sunday it is tradition and law that everyone must attend church. Again, the homes are all checked, and offenders who are found not to be in church are fined. Families are likewise fined when their children break the law or fail to uphold their responsibilities as good citizens, so strong moral traditions are ingrained in Samoan life. In this way, moral or common law provides more actual control on the island than do governmental laws. Because of these things, Toe grew up with a definite sense of right and wrong and developed an outstanding character.

Though her childhood and teenage years were filled with religious influence, Toe tried to avoid the Mormon Church and its missionaries for as long as possible. When she first met the missionaries they represented to her a drastic change from her already secure and comfortable life. After all, her stepfather was a minister in another church. But the missionaries persisted, finding ways to accidentally "run into" her. They even talked with Toe's sister to find out if Toe had any interest in the Church at all! I would think they would have been discouraged, because they were assured that there was no way that Toe would consider their church.

Toe told me that she'd walk the long way home just to avoid the missionaries, because she knew they'd be waiting for her. In Samoa the people often carry umbrellas to protect themselves from the sun, and when Toe saw the missionaries coming she'd flip up her umbrella to hide her face from them.

For some reason the missionaries felt Toe would be a golden contact if they could just talk to her long enough to explain the gospel. The missionary who eventually baptized her decided he'd played hide-and-go-seek with her long enough, so one day he hid in some bushes along a walkway she usually traveled on her way home. His persistence paid off, for when she came down the walk that day, he suddenly appeared from the bushes. What could she say then? It's a little awkward to be out-and-out rude to someone when they're standing right in front of you.

They began to teach Toe the gospel, and I'm glad they did, for on October 26, 1968, she was baptized. She didn't waste any time getting involved in the Church from that point on. The following year, on December 11, 1969, she received her endowments in the New Zealand Temple, and from 1970 to 1972 she served a full-time mission in the Samoan Islands.

It seems that Toe's life prior to coming in contact with Mormonism prepared her to accept the gospel; and, of course, I feel that each portion of my own life was another step leading me to eventual recognition of the truthfulness of the gospel. And this wasn't the only thing we had in common. Toe's whole life was religiously oriented and so was mine; her family practiced the laws of charity and love of all men, and so did mine; Toe came from humble but honest parents—everyone in the family contributed in some way to the stability and well-being of the family—and I came from equally humble beginnings. In Samoa Toe gained love and appreciation for nature and the land, and as I've already said, I'm a country boy through and through. The longer we lived together, the greater and more significant kinds of things we found in common. Though at first glance our marriage had seemed like the impossible dream, in reality our similarities far outnumbered our differences.

I don't mean to suggest that we didn't have our challenges, though. Of course we did, and most centered around our difference in race and culture. On the whole, we felt accepted by other Church members in our ward. Being a black Mormon was a bit of a novelty, and I found myself being asked to speak in many wards across the island. I certainly wasn't ignored, and by the time I left Hawaii I had spoken in nearly every chapel on the island of Oahu.

I was called to be the teacher development director in our ward. There was a little embarrassment associated with this calling, though, for as I read the manual outlining my responsibilities I realized that this position was to be filled by a Melchizedek Priesthood holder. I pointed this out to my bishop, who was also a little embarrassed. But when he realized that I wasn't offended by this mistake, my calling was changed to teacher development teacher, which seemed completely in line with Church policy. I was also asked to home teach, though the stake president in Hawaii asked that I accompany two other elders. And I also attended elders quorum meetings and was often asked to substitute as the teacher.

Toe was put to work in our ward as quickly as I was, so we did feel fellowship and a sense of belonging there. Of course, there are those whose prejudices kept them from freely and openly welcoming us into the fold. Some of my most uncomfortable moments were spent as I waited to pick Toe up from the college. Others who were waiting found it difficult to even acknowledge me. It is a little frustrating to walk right up to somebody to whom you have been introduced and say hello, only to receive a blank stare in return or perhaps a hasty nod of the head.

I worried about Toe more than I worried about myself, though, because I was reared in an era when black people were still treated as inferior, uneducated, unthinking, lowly beings. Many times in my childhood and teenage days I entered a restaurant from the "Negro entrance" or sat in the back of the bus or waited an hour to be served in a cafe. I had learned what prejudice was, and I had learned that the last thing I needed was to worry about those who chose to dislike me. But Toe hadn't experienced those pressures. This was a new experience for her, and as you can imagine it is difficult to be married to somebody whom others esteem to be undesirable and inferior. I knew I had to strengthen her somehow; there's nothing pleasant about being shunned because of your choice of marriage partner. Yet I, who was the cause of her embarrassment, was at a loss to know how to provide her with the support and inner strength she needed—or at least that I felt she needed.

But Toe was stronger than I gave her credit for. Oh, I'm sure that she spent anxious hours reconciling within herself the tension created by rude remarks, apathetic stares, and a plain lack of manners on the part of some. Her commitment to me was firm, however—I am so thankful for that!—and her knowledge that the Lord had sanctioned our marriage gave her the strength to rise above these challenges.

I decided before we ever got married that I'd better do my part to keep the romance alive in our marriage, which seemed like an enjoyable challenge to me! Especially since Toe was far from her homeland and family, I felt a need to provide her with a solid foundation of our own and to give her certain choices in planning our life together. For example, many of the problems I've seen occur in intercultural marriages have been because the wife was lonely and homesick. So I decided when we first got married that Toe could name the place where she most wanted to live. She chose Samoa, and I agreed. I immediately began making plans and setting goals that would allow us within a relatively short number of years to take our family back to Samoa. Some might say that's a large concession to make, but I knew before I ever married Toe that I'd have to willingly make sacrifices to keep our marriage happy and alive. And to me, this is a small sacrifice to make if it means knowing that my wife is happy.

Being the lover's paradise that it is, Hawaii provided the perfect setting for our first two months of marriage. We visited the beach and parks and national monuments—the whole atmosphere was at the same time exciting and invigorating, yet peaceful and tranquil. We laughed and enjoyed carefree moments of finding out about each other and of falling more completely in love with each other. And this would have continued had it not been for one minor little detail—Toe left me.

Toe didn't *leave* me, as she would have in breaking up our marriage, but in late August she had the opportunity to fly to Samoa to visit her mother for a week or so. We both knew that it might be a while before another chance would come for her to visit home, so I took her to the airport, consoling myself that she'd only be gone a couple of weeks.

Well, two weeks came and went—and no Toe. I was almost at the point of being upset when I received word from her that somehow, by our own oversight, her visa had expired while she was in Samoa, and she was having trouble getting it renewed. It seems that the red tape in Samoa's emigration department was in its usual confusing condition, and the backlog of Samoans waiting for visas was at an all-time high.

I thought that surely all would be resolved within a few days, but September came and went, October dragged by, and when I found myself eating Thanksgiving dinner by myself, my patience ran out. I arranged for an immediate leave from the army, and one day during the first week in December I found myself on a plane bound for Western Samoa. Toe didn't know I was coming, and I had only the post office box number of a friend she was staying with to help me locate her. But I just couldn't endure staying in Hawaii any longer where I was useless to help my wife.

In my haste to leave Hawaii I never even stopped to think that I'd need a passport, so when I landed in Pago Pago in American Samoa (where a passport is not needed, since it is an American dependency), I found that I could not go on to Western Samoa. *How stupid can I be?* I thought to myself, frustrated that now not only was Toe in a jam, but I'd worked myself into quite a situation as well.

I always say that the Lord works in mysterious ways, but this time he surprised even me. I was wandering around the air terminal, looking lost, when a gentleman driving a tour car tapped me on the shoulder and asked if he could give me directions. Within a minute I had spilled my story, and would you believe it—he was a member of the Church, and he knew just how to help me! He grabbed my arm and we hustled around the airport from one little department to another. Before I knew it, I had a three-day temporary passport and was free to go as I pleased. This good man then took me to a friend of his—

another member of the Church—who was (very conveniently, I thought) a taxi driver. He proceeded to drive me all over the island, stopping at several places where I needed to go to get the three-day passport finalized. He even took me to his home for dinner and to meet his family. Later that evening he drove me back to the airport to catch the flight to Apia, the capital of Western Samoa.

When I was finally in the air again, this time with passport in hand, who should I meet but two Mormon missionaries? I didn't let on that I was a member of the Church, which made for a very interesting conversation. As we were preparing to land, one of the missionaries happened to remark that a young lady by the name of Isapela Leituala had taught him in the Language Training Center at the Church College of Hawaii. I'm sure he wondered why such a shocked expression came over my face, and of course I had to tell them then that the same Isapela Leituala was my wife and that I was a member of the Church.

Upon arriving in Apia on the island of Upolu in Western Samoa, I immediately took a cab and began looking for Toe with only the post office box number for a clue. Late that evening I had failed to come up with an address for Toe (the post office box number did me little good in finding her), so I told the cab driver to take me to the mission home, which he did.

There I ran into another stroke of luck—of course, I know better than to really think it was only luck. I just happened to walk into a party that was being held at one of the Church schools right behind the mission home, and there *just happened* to be a couple there whom I'd met months earlier at the Cultural Center in Hawaii. And they *just happened* to know Toe's brother-in-law, who was a bishop in a local ward.

These friends took me home with them for the night, and the following morning they took me to Toe's brother-in-law's home; it was the first contact I'd had with any member of Toe's family. Toe's brother-in-law knew about her visa dilemma, and she *just happened* to be at that moment staying with her brother. So he rushed me over to the brother's house where, after four long months, Toe and I were reunited.

When I walked into the house Toe's jaw fell open and then, of course, she started to cry. I can't remember when I've felt as happy and relieved as I did at that moment!

After the excitement of seeing each other again had calmed down a little, Toe gave me a formal introduction to her family. I'd been so concerned about finding Toe that I hadn't stopped to worry about meeting her family. After all, I was black, and that is not always the most popular color to be in Samoa. But I did have one thing working in my favor. In Samoa ministers occupy a very respected position and are honored by the people. I had been a minister at one time, so that was a plus for me. And I had converted to Mormonism, and Toe had several relatives who had also converted and who were very active in the Church.

We all really enjoyed the short time we spent with each other. I got to meet two of Toe's brothers, her sister and brother-in-law, and an uncle, who was the high chief of the family. Before Toe and I left Samoa, the family even held a feast in my honor. And they really went whole hog, to coin a phrase, by killing a pig and roasting it on hot rocks in the umu. I sat on a grass mat, ate taro and coconut, felt the ocean breezes, and tasted succulent roast pork. It was all as delightful as Toe had described it.

But though I'd found Toe and met her family we still had a problem—Toe didn't have a visa. She'd waited in long lines day after day trying to get her papers cleared. Again we were helped by a member of the Church, who *just happened* to know one of the officials who issued visas. And this official *just happened* to be a member of the Church as well. He told us to come to his office the next day. When we arrived, the official called Toe to the head of the line, dug her paperwork out from underneath a stack of visa applications, and okayed her request. So in a matter of a couple of hours, everything was taken care of. It seems that from the beginning of my rush trip to Samoa I'd been blessed with fortunate "coincidences." Now, we could go home!

A week from the day I'd landed in Samoa without a passport or a wife, I headed back for Hawaii, the proud possessor of both. And once back in Hawaii, we resumed our honeymoon, enjoying once again the beauty Hawaii had to offer and the companionship of one another. And by this time our joy had taken on a new dimension, for we had found that we were going to have a baby.

But our honeymoon in Hawaii was bound to come to an end. By February of 1975 I had had enough of the army, and I'm sure they were tired of me. My three-year obligation to them was taken care of. Since our first baby was due in March, we began to make plans to leave Hawaii after the baby was born and Toe was back on her feet. I wanted my family to meet and get acquainted with Toe; then we had to settle down, begin to make a living, and financially prepare for the move to Samoa.

We talked long about where we would both most like to live in the states, and after tossing several ideas around we decided that Salt Lake City was first choice. Toe thought it would be great to live so close to the prophet. The center of the Church had always seemed so far away to her, especially since her entire association with the Church had been in Hawaii and Samoa; she wanted to be where ''the fire was burning,'' as she put it.

I was a little less anxious to move to Utah, where I wondered if we might find it a little ''cold''—and I wasn't referring to the weather. I knew there weren't many black people—members *or* nonmembers—in Utah, and I could just see us each Sunday morning in a sea of white faces I feared might be unfriendly.

I had been told about the Genesis group that was functioning in the Salt Lake Valley for black members of the Church, and that did appeal to me. In Hawaii I knew of only two other Negro members of the Church, and they had joined the Church after I did. So the Genesis group was a definite plus in Salt Lake's favor. When I then made a deal with a contractor to work with him in Salt Lake building homes, the decision seemed easy to make.

It's exciting and even a little frightening to await the birth of your first child, but the eagerly anticipated day finally arrived when, on March 12, Toe gave birth to our first little boy, Alexander Fuamai. Holding my little boy was a joy beyond belief! Yet I couldn't help but ache inside a few weeks later when I had to hand him over to another man—an elder—so he could receive his name and a blessing. Tears fell freely and pain seared my heart during the moments I allowed myself to dwell on the fact that I could not bless my own son. But I turned my thoughts to the blessing afforded me by my membership in the Church. There was no sense in dwelling on a restriction I could not change, and I did know how very fortunate I was to be one of the relatively few who had found the gospel.

We had a few months to adjust to our new little family member, for Toe to regain her health, and for all of us to enjoy those last weeks of beautiful Hawaii. By autumn of that year all arrangements had been made, and we felt that it was time to enter a new phase of our life. So in October of 1975 we left Hawaii with the intention of first spending several months with my family in North Carolina and then heading for the West, a place unknown and unfamiliar to both of us.

It was hard to leave Hawaii. What a turning point those islands had been in my life! Three years earlier an innocent, single, country-boy-turned-Holiness-minister had flown in, eager and willing to make his fortune. Now, an older (and, I hope, wiser) married Mormon was boarding the plane. Hawaii had proved to be the turning point of my whole life—probably in my whole eternal destiny. The only way I could explain it to myself, I thought, as the plane lifted up over the beautiful beaches and headed east into the clouds, was that the Lord does work in mysterious ways. I could only hope that the Lord's direction and guidance would be with me in the years to come as it had been in Hawaii.

Private Joseph Freeman, 1972.

Joseph, Toe, Alexander, and Zechariah pose on the steps of the Salt Lake Temple on June 23, 1978, after having been sealed as a family.
—*Photo by Eldon K. Linschoten*

Proud father displays month-old Isapela following blessing ceremony, while Bishop Karl H. Glover watches.

Bearing testimony while holding adopted daughter Moana.

Family picture, 1979: clockwise—Moana, Toe, Joseph, Isapela, Zechariah, Alexander.

Home in
the Valley

I don't think Toe enjoyed one minute of the flight from Hawaii to North Carolina. The butterflies were dancing too rapidly in her stomach. After all, this was more than just her first trip to the continental United States: she would soon be meeting her in-laws for the first time. Though I wasn't worried at all about the "big introduction," Toe felt the emotions everyone does as they are preparing to get inspected by the partner's family. And I'm sure she was extra apprehensive, not knowing quite what to expect from her Negro husband's family.

As usually happens, the worrying was in vain, because she loved my family and they thought she was just terrific. Mother was especially pleased and relieved to see that I'd married a religious girl, for that had been her biggest concern. And our little five-month-old son Alexander was a real hit with the family—the apple of his grandparents' eye.

It was great to be home! It seemed like an eternity since I had been with my family, and it's always a shock to find that your younger brothers and sisters have grown up. For several days I just took everything in—the beauty of North Carolina, familiar streets and favorite places, the little church I used to attend, old friends, my mother and father.

There's a certain homesickness or longing you feel when you come home and find that things will never be quite the same as they were before. The willows don't seem quite as tall, the ice cream's not as cold, the dirt roads don't have quite the lure they did for an eight-year-old barefoot boy. As much as I loved my new life, I found my mind racing over memories of my boyhood. Beginning to feel the demands which fatherhood had brought me, my appreciation for my own parents was intensified. So my experience back in North Carolina was filled with good times, deep emotions, and dreams for the future.

It was especially interesting to be back in the surroundings where I had for so long planned and worked to become a minister. My most meaningful childhood memories centered around my family and the many church-related things we did together—choir practices, singing together around the piano, lying under the oak tree while reading of my Bible heroes, watching Mother preach from the pulpit, feeling security in Dad's quiet but commanding counsel. Now, with added insight and a new perspective on all that is really important, I found myself taking a closer look at my good parents and others there who were such devout believers in Jesus Christ.

Though the gospel had taught me full truths, I could still see in my old Holiness faith many worthwhile ideals, and I really felt that the people who worshipped in this manner were sincere and genuinely filled with the Spirit many times. This confused me. I knew the gospel to be true, yet how could members from two different churches both have prayers answered and feel the presence of the Spirit in their lives if one church was undoubtedly the only church of Christ upon the earth? Without meaning to, I began to compare my old faith with the Church, and I sought answers to these questions.

I knew my parents were sincere in their worship; I also knew them to be genuinely good Christian people who tried to pattern their lives after Christ. My mind and heart told me, though, that my newly found religion was Christ's true church, and therefore the only one on the earth today receiving divine sanction and guidance.

My good wife came to the rescue, for she could tell that I needed this resolved in my mind—especially while we were on my home turf, where the influence of the past was the most real. One evening she put a question to me: "I know you've been able to feel the Spirit working in your life for as long as you can remember, so obviously you were sensitive to the promptings of the Spirit before you were a member of the Church. But have you also been taught by the Spirit that this gospel is the church of Christ?"

Of course I had! Suddenly things began to clear in my mind. All people are born with the light of Christ, and with that light they can respond to the promptings of truth and light—if they allow themselves to respond.

It wouldn't be fair to think that those who had not yet found the gospel were not entitled to some heavenly promptings and guidance. It's just that those who have accepted the gospel message and have therefore received the gift of the Holy Ghost have a special line of communication with the Savior, for the Holy Ghost acts as their channel to the Father and Son. All of the puzzle pieces fit into place—thank heavens! It was almost a relief to understand how my mother and father had lived righteous lives and were sincere in their beliefs, though they had not done so within the gospel plan. I knew that they were good people, and yet the concept of the "only true Church" had always troubled me when I thought of them and others in their situation. I now felt at peace.

It was after I had resolved this nagging question and while we were still in North Carolina that our little family had a stirring and surprising experience. One day Alexander became very sick. Medicine, visits to the doctor, and tender loving care didn't seem to help, so we finally contacted a Mormon bishop we knew and asked that he administer to Alexander.

The bishop began the blessing in the usual way, but about half-way through the blessing he paused, and with some hesitation, continued on: "Alexander, you will regain your health and strength and will one day serve a mission for the Church."

My heart nearly stopped! How could that be? Alexander obviously had me for a father, and I was obviously darker than those who were allowed to hold the priesthood—a necessary requirement for being called on a mission. I don't think I heard another word of the blessing, and Toe was even more excited.

The bishop had scarcely said "Amen" before Toe was asking him what he had meant. After being bombarded with a series of questions, his only explanation was, "I don't know why I said it, except that I felt inspired to."

I didn't know what to think of the bishop's remark; I only felt I shouldn't dwell upon a mystery. And really, the whole priesthood issue didn't disturb me very often. As a matter of fact, I came to realize that any negative feelings I had were only an attempt by evil forces to put a dent in my protective armor. And with a black Mormon, what was a more sensitive issue than the priesthood? When I finally realized what was happening, my doubts and frustrations subsided and I felt strengthened for having gone through the experience.

The only times after that experience that I worried about the Negro/priesthood question were in relationship to my young son, the baby Toe was now carrying, and any other children the Lord would bless us with. I felt the need to be able to bless them and to be able to bless our home. And though I often offered prayers of faith when Toe or Alexander were ill or had special concerns, I was well aware that that was just what they were—prayers of faith. There was no way that I could invoke the special power of the priesthood to be with my family.

And I also looked ahead to the time when my boy would turn twelve years old. The time was bound to come when his peers and friends would stand in front of the sacrament table and go to deacons quorum meetings together. Would Alexander be firm enough in his self-esteem and in his testimony that this would not bother him? Maybe it would tug at my heart more than his; but I wasn't looking forward to that time. Somehow I had to provide such a strong spiritual background in our home that as my children grew and faced these challenges, despite any peer pressure or frustration they would feel they would not be able to deny the truth. The thought of one of my children straying from the Church tore at my heart like nothing ever had before.

I supposed the only solution to this question that plagues all parents was to just dig in and do all I could to provide my family with a quality home. I was finding that there's nothing quite like having your own child to add purpose and meaning to life—as well as emphasizing the responsibility of providing, in every sense of the word.

After several months at home, both Toe and I felt the urgency of moving on and establishing our family. In the first weeks of March, I again waved good-bye to North Carolina as we bid our adieus and set out to establish our family in Salt Lake City.

A Moslem on his first pilgrimage to Mecca or a Jew having his first glance at the Wailing Wall probably feels the same awe and thrill that I—a recently converted Mormon—did that first day in Salt Lake City. The Brigham Young statue, the This Is the Place Monument, the Lion House and Eagle Gate, and the impressive twenty-eight-story Church Office Building swept us into the mainstream of Church history—past and present.

And the only thing that can be said about Temple Square is that it is magnificent! I wanted to spend hours there—listening to the Tabernacle Choir rehearse; contemplating my own relationship to Christ as I viewed the *Christus*; gaining just an inkling of the slogan, "Worldwide Church," through the exhibits at the visitor's center; dwelling upon the joy our Savior must have in these symbols of respect for him; and partaking of the calm, tranquil spiritual aura that pervades Temple Square.

And, of course, it was almost a culture shock to come from an area where Mormonism is unheard of by many and unembraced by most to a city where a chapel or stake center dots almost every other city block.

As we found an apartment to rent and settled down to everyday living, both Toe and I began to realize that beneath the veneer of the tremendous Church activity, and though the Mormon Church definitely had its roots in the Salt Lake Valley, there were many more nonmembers than we would have ever supposed. And perhaps even more startling was the number of inactive members of the Church we came in contact with daily. How someone could live right here, in the presence of the leaders of the Church—at the very heart of Zion—and become careless in his commitment to the gospel was something I could not at first understand. I was disappointed in the obvious apathy of some members and inactive members until it dawned on me that if this spiritual numbness could overtake others, it could overtake me as well—and that I'd better make sure that it didn't. Besides, what a great opportunity for missionary work! Actually, we really had the best of both worlds here: the advantages of enjoying the strength of the Church in Utah and the challenge to bring the others into the fold all in one.

As we began to attend our ward my fears about a chilly reception faded away. Though in one ward we didn't receive home teachers for about a year, I'm sure that was no reflection on us but just on the lukewarm attitude of those particular home teachers. And we had enough love from those who did fellowship and welcome us into the ward to make up for those who chose not to. Whenever I've felt that my race was creating a negative reaction or uncomfortable situation, I've learned to rely upon the scripture from the words of Paul when he said that "[nothing] shall be able to separate us from the love of God" (Romans 8:39). We certainly never felt alienated from His love or even from the acceptance of fellow Church members.

I couldn't help but chuckle, though, on our first Sunday morning in Salt Lake. As I walked into elders quorum meeting, as I had been doing regularly since my baptism, the gentleman at the door stared at me and then stammered, "I'm glad to see you attending our meetings with us." I'm sure he'd never seen a Negro in priesthood meeting before, and I could see that I'd completely flustered him. But I'd been asked by my first stake president to attend priesthood meeting with the other elders, and it never dawned on me that my attendance might be a surprise to others elsewhere. My bishop in this new ward extended the same invitation to me, and after a while I think everyone got used to seeing me walk through the door each Sunday morning.

We'd been in Salt Lake only a couple of months when we prepared to welcome our second son into the world. I was thrilled at the prospect of having a second child! Alexander was absolutely my pride and joy—talk about a pushover, I took the cake.

We'd barely managed to get settled in Salt Lake when our second baby decided it was time to make his entrance. Our second son, Zechariah Tuimavave, was born on May 20, 1976. Toe and I had been blessed with two of the most beautiful sons in as many years. (Of course, I'm not prejudiced.) I couldn't believe my luck—actually, I again knew that it wasn't luck at all, but a very real blessing.

As our little family grew I felt an increasing sense of fulfillment within. I began to realize that a lifetime dream was actually coming to fruition. I had always wanted to be part of a Mormon family—though of course, I hadn't always known that. I had always wanted my family life to be built around the gospel; not only did I now have the beginning of my family, but I had *the* gospel, the Church of Jesus Christ.

I did feel, though, the desire and the need to associate with other members of my race—particularly those who had also embraced the Church. I had never forgotten what I'd been told back in Hawaii about the black LDS group that met in Salt Lake City. Ever since Toe and I had arrived in Utah I'd made inquiries about the Genesis group, but it seemed that no one knew any reliable details about its organization or even where and when it met. There was nothing listed in the phone book under that name, and not even my bishop or stake president could direct me to them. I was finally told that the group didn't actually exist, but that it was a myth that had somehow been circulated throughout the Church. Disappointed, I pushed the whole thing from my mind.

In 1977 we moved to a different part of Salt Lake which meant, of course, that we became members of a different ward. We'd only been there a week or two when the bishop, Jay H. Swain, approached me and said, "I guess you're aware of the Genesis group and have been meeting with them."

I blinked my eyes in surprise and told him of the difficulty I'd had in even finding out if the Genesis group actually existed. Bishop Swain knew the president of the Genesis group, Ruffin Bridgeforth, and immediately put me in touch with him. We were told of an upcoming Christmas party the group was having and finally, late in 1977, we were introduced to this group of people I'd been searching for ever since we moved to Salt Lake.

In the Genesis group we found a place where we felt additional purpose, responsibility, and a sense of belonging. It had always bothered me that so few of my people had found and then accepted the gospel. I knew that if the gospel was true, then it was true for everyone. I'd worried many hours about coming up with a way to somehow bring, on a large scale, the light of the gospel to the black population. Now I could tell that the Genesis group would provide the setting where this could happen.

The Genesis group was organized in 1971 under the direction of the Council of the Twelve to provide a place of worship and fellowship for black members of the Church. It has always functioned under the direction of the president of the Salt Lake Liberty Stake, and has grown significantly since its creation.

Because there is not a large black population in the Salt Lake Valley (or in Utah, for that matter), we found that some who attended the group were not members of the Church, but had somehow found out about this group of black people who met together. The Genesis group provided us with otherwise-hard-to-come-by missionary contacts.

Students (both members and nonmembers) from the University of Utah and from Brigham Young University attended, as did others who happened to be in Salt Lake on business or other purposes for short periods of time. One night we were surprised by a phone call from a doctor in California who had heard about our group. He had his own plane and wanted to fly down the next evening for a meeting to hear about the gospel and to meet other black members of the Church. He was not a member, but had been interested in the Church for some time; the priesthood restriction had been a roadblock, however, and he was curious to see how those who had already embraced the gospel had resolved it in their minds and lives.

We associated with the group for a month or so when the president, Ruffin Bridgeforth, asked if I would accompany him and his counselors on speaking engagements in other wards and at firesides. I felt honored to travel with them, representing our group and the Church. Once again I had the thrill of standing behind the pulpit preaching the gospel—similar to experiences I'd had during my minister days in the Holiness Church. Of course, the difference I felt while speaking was amazing; when I earnestly sought the Spirit to bless my thoughts and words, I could feel that assurance and power as I spoke. Maybe I couldn't hold the priesthood and participate in the "ministry" of my new church, but that didn't have to keep me from bearing testimony and perhaps adding to the conviction and knowledge of others.

Toe and I were both enjoying both our ward and the Genesis group when, in May of 1976, I received a call that the stake president wanted to talk with my wife and me. *What have I done this time?* was my first thought. I couldn't imagine what he wanted to speak to *me* for. With a little fear and a little more trembling we kept our appointment with him; my worst fears proved to be rather silly when he asked Toe if she'd be willing to support me and if I'd be willing to serve as the second counselor in the Genesis presidency.

Willing to serve? I was overwhelmed! This seemed about as close as I would ever come to serving in a leadership or "ministerial" position in the Church, and I was thrilled. President Bridgeforth and his first counselor, James Dawson (who sings in the Tabernacle Choir), were such outstanding men. What a challenge it would be to live up to their expectations and bring the same quality leadership to the group! I knew of a time in the past when the group had needed steadfast leadership and direction. In fact, when we first attended the Christmas party in December 1977, there were only a handful of members, as the group had only a short time earlier suffered a serious split.

About a year before Toe and I had been introduced to the Genesis group, division and disharmony had thundered through the group, dividing the wheat from the tares, so to speak. In 1976 an elder in the Church living in Vancouver, Washington, took it upon himself to baptize a black man and then "ordain" him to the priesthood. This action was not sanctioned by the First Presidency, and when the elder refused to cooperate with Church officials by renouncing his claim of authority to officiate in such an ordination, he was excommunicated from the Church.

The entire incident encouraged some of the Genesis members to get their grievances off their chests by openly criticizing the leaders of the Church for their failure to acknowledge equality of its black members by revoking the priesthood restriction. Arguments, dissension, and heated debates resulted; some were so insistent that they drew up a petition for all in the group to sign demanding that President Spencer W. Kimball modify previous statements on interracial marriage and make a firm commitment as to when the priesthood would be given to the Negro people. Most, of course, would not sign this petition; but quite a few did—enough to cause a damaging split in the group.

When the petition was presented to President Bridgeforth, he stood firm in his support of the policies of the Church and particularly of the prophet and the other General Authorities. When the dissenters could see that their rebellion was not supported by their immediate leaders, they left the group in disgust. Some who had not supported the petition also left, not wanting to be part of a group where this kind of contention existed. It was so discouraging for all involved in the group to see it cut in half because of the successful efforts of the adversary—and especially when it was just gaining momentum and strength. Those whose foundation was built upon sand had truly fallen, but those whose testimonies were based upon correct principles and truth had remained loyal to the Church.

The Genesis group did begin to rebuild and regain strength; but now, as I contemplated my new calling, my heart ached for those who had not been able to see the forest for the trees and who had let their preoccupation with a ''cause'' blind them to the truth and to the Spirit of the Lord. I wanted more than anything else to be an example to my people so that in future times of trial we would be able to stand firm together.

I knew, though, that in order to strengthen others, I had to first fortify and strengthen myself and my own family. Each new day of marriage and fatherhood brought with it a renewed determination to improve the quality of our home. And the covenant I had made with my Father as I had contemplated my marriage to Toe was never far from my mind. I had dedicated my family to the Lord, and when that dedication involves quality day-to-day living, it is a pretty tall order. I had taken this responsibility upon myself knowing full well that the priesthood would not bless our home as we sought exaltation together, and each addition to the family made me realize more fully the scope and breadth of living everyday life in harmony with gospel principles.

The year 1977 brought us another addition to the family, though this addition came in a little different manner. Alexander and Zechariah finally had a little sister, but the burden of childbearing was relieved from Toe as we adopted a darling little baby girl, whom we named Moana Marie.

Daily I expressed gratitude to the Lord for his plan that allows us to live and love and grow in family units. Time only made me love Toe more. Her influence on the growth of our children was inestimable; sometimes I would pinch myself just to make sure I really was married to her and that we already had three fantastic children. The first four years of marriage were for us years of growth, sacrifice, and adaptability. After all, learning to put a roast in the oven rather than wrapping it in banana leaves and placing it on hot rocks in the umu was quite an adjustment for Toe. And I dreamed up everything conceivable to put little sparks of excitement into our marriage so that Toe would be less likely to get homesick or to wonder if she'd done the right thing.

Then, of course, children by their very nature bring with them the challenge to practice unconditional love and patience and to spend less time worrying about yourself. Parents automatically get second billing when children are involved.

But all of these things only resulted in greater love and commitment between Toe and me. Our whole family's commitment to gospel principles increased as we saw how their application made a difference in the caliber of our life at home. There was only one thing that nagged at me—when I would let it. The greater my love for Toe and the kids grew, the more desirous and anxious I became to have them sealed to me for time and all eternity. Who knew what could happen the very next day? One hates to be a pessimistic bearer of gloomy predictions, but the thought of losing a member of my family was almost more than I could bear.

One thing made this easier, though, and that was knowing that God was just. Surely some provisions would be made for us to live eternally together. Since the time I joined the Church I had always felt that a way would be provided so that my family wouldn't be penalized for my personal limitation. If I hadn't had this assurance in my heart, I might never have joined the Church.

It was always my determination to live worthy of holding the priesthood so that if and when that blessing was given to me, there would be nothing in terms of personal worthiness that could stand in my way.

At Last
a Minister

You know how it is when you watch a movie or read a book where everyone doesn't end up living happily ever after? Do you ever pretend that things really turned out all right? I must be a romanticist, because I can't stand it if the good guys don't win, the couple doesn't fall in love, or the hero doesn't rescue the damsel in distress—all in the nick of time, of course.

Who would have ever dreamed that I would witness and even play a minor role in one of the greatest "happily ever afters" of modern times? That June morning in 1978 I had awakened feeling no different than I had felt the day before. The lawn needed watering and weeding, just as it had when I had gone to bed the night before; yesterday's newspaper was still on the living room floor; and Toe had several things around the house I needed to fix before leaving for work. Everything was basically as it always was.

In a matter of only a couple of hours, however, every semblance of normalcy left our little family. There was no way I could have known, of course, that for a long while the leaders of the Church—particularly the prophet—had been pleading with the Lord for guidance concerning my people. A temple was under construction and would soon be dedicated in Sao Paulo, Brazil, a multiracial area. The number of black members of the Church was increasing only slowly, partly because of black males being denied the priesthood; yet missionary work to take the gospel to all nations and peoples was being increasingly accelerated, which would mean active proselyting among the black populations of the world. These faithful black Church members were being held back from temple blessings. These and, I'm sure, many other factors caused President Kimball and other General Authorities to plead fervently with the Lord in behalf of the Negro people.

Now the Lord had made a direct response to these earnest and numerous pleadings, and this had been made known to Church leaders everywhere in the following letter, dated June 8, 1978:

Dear Brethren:

As we have witnessed the expansion of the work of the Lord over the earth, we have been grateful that people of many nations have responded to the message of the restored gospel, and have joined the church in ever-increasing numbers. This, in turn, has inspired us with a desire to extend to every worthy member of the church all of the privileges and blessings which the gospel affords.

Aware of the promises made by the prophets and presidents of the church who have preceded us that at some time, in God's eternal plan, all of our brethren who are worthy may receive the priesthood, and witnessing the faithfulness of those from whom the priesthood has been withheld, we have pleaded long and earnestly in behalf of these, our faithful brethren, spending many hours in the upper room of the Temple supplicating the Lord for divine guidance.

He has heard our prayers, and by revelation has confirmed that the long-promised day has come when every faithful, worthy man in the church may receive the holy priesthood, with power to exercise its divine authority, and enjoy with his loved ones every blessing that flows therefrom, including the blessings of the temple. Accordingly, all worthy male members of the church may be ordained to the priesthood without regard for race or color. Priesthood leaders are instructed to follow the policy of carefully interviewing all candidates for ordination to either the Aaronic or Melchizedek Priesthood to insure that they meet the established standards for worthiness.

We declare with soberness that the Lord has now made known his will for the blessing of all his children throughout the earth who will hearken to the voice of his authorized servants, and prepare themselves to receive every blessing of the gospel.

Sincerely yours,

Spencer W. Kimball
N. Eldon Tanner
Marion G. Romney

Thus on June 9, 1978, a day that began like any other, that exciting and timely revelation was announced to the world. And only two days later, on June 11, hands were placed upon my head and I was ordained an elder in the Holy Melchizedek Priesthood.

What a difference a day makes! All those years that I'd desired more than anything else to be a minister! And the ministerial days that had followed, when I had known I lacked something that a true messenger of God should have. Then to give up being a minister for membership in a church where I was plummeted to the bottom of the ecclesiastical totem pole! But now—finally—my elusive dream had come true! I had been found worthy to receive the greatest power bestowed on man!

I'm sure I would have walked around in a trance for several days if I hadn't been the object of so much excitement, curiosity, and genuine interest. By some quirk, I had managed to be the first black man ordained to the priesthood, and when such a newsworthy story breaks, you can't begin to imagine the assortment of people who suddenly come out of the woodwork—newspaper reporters, magazine editors, freelance writers, television news commentators. I found my face being flashed across newspapers, on the evening news, even in magazines—I was almost afraid it would turn up on the front of some T-shirt somewhere. And not only were local news agencies interested in the story, but on Tuesday, only two days after I was ordained, I received a call from an agent representing ''Good Morning

America,'' the morning television show hosted by David Hartman. They wanted me to appear on their show the very next morning. I was overwhelmed; there's no other way to put it! I realized, of course, that I was merely a symbol of this great event in our Church's history, but I felt humbled and honored—plus a great sense of responsibility to represent the Church well to the rest of the world.

My experience on "Good Morning, America" was a memorable one. David Hartman was the perfect host, and I felt gratified to express on national television my thoughts and thankfulness about receiving the priesthood.

I'm sure Toe felt like my receptionist for a while as we set up appointments with writers, newsmen, photographers, and the host of other media-associated people who sought our time. I couldn't imagine that so many people wanted to talk to me. I was interviewed by writers for *Time, Ebony,* and *People* magazines. One newspaper editor from Australia even flew in to see me. The phone rang day and night. One morning I answered it at 6:00 A.M. only to find myself on the air with a disc jockey from California who wanted his listeners to hear about my ordination "straight from the horse's mouth."

Before even a week or two had elapsed, our phone began ringing off the wall with invitations for Toe and me to speak to wards, firesides, MIA groups, and stake conferences. Of course we were happy and willing to share our testimonies of the gospel, but it seemed a little curious to me that I would be the focus of so much attention. There were plenty of other equally worthy Negro brethren who'd also received the priesthood, many of whom I'm sure were better speakers and who were more exemplary men than I. But being the "first" in anything makes for instant celebrities, and Toe and I entered into a very hectic schedule, often attending two or three sacrament meetings and a couple of firesides on a single Sunday. At one point we were scheduled solid for six months in advance.

The attention and jam-packed schedule, however, brought the least amount of change to our lives. The greatest impact of my ordination was a much more meaningful, significant, and far-reaching one. Not only would my priesthood allow me to bless the lives of my children and wife, but I now had the privilege of receiving my blessings in the house of the Lord. I was no longer the cause for holding Toe or my children back. Our family could be sealed together as an eternal family!

As I contemplated this, the realization of what was about to take place overwhelmed me to the point that I was no longer in control of my emotions. Tears streamed freely down my face and my heart was bursting with love for my Heavenly Father, who had made this possible, and for my family, who meant more to me than mortal words could ever express. How grateful I was that, four years earlier, I had listened to the words of my bishop, who had counseled me to let Toe make the decision about our marriage! I would never again have to feel that I had deprived Toe of something she was worthy of.

The day I received the priesthood, Bishop Swain advised Toe and me to not delay in taking our family to the temple. Our house was now a center of excitement and preparation! The children caught on to Toe's and my enthusiasm as we all looked forward to that day. And there were humorous as well as spiritual experiences associated with preparation to go to the temple.

On the morning that Toe called the temple to schedule a time for our family to be sealed, she sat Alexander and Zechariah down and explained to them what was going to happen.

"On Friday we're all going to the temple to be sealed together for time and eternity," Toe said.

Alexander looked at her with a puzzled expression and replied, "But Mommy, the seal is not in the temple, it's in the zoo." Toe chuckled all morning about that one, as I did in the evening when she told me about it. This was going to be a new experience for all of us.

On the morning of June 23, 1978—two weeks after the announcement—we piled the children in the car and headed for probably the most important appointment we'd ever keep. As we drove to Temple Square I was flooded with memories of some of the stories I'd heard as a little boy about my relatives. Great-grandpa Freeman had to "jump the broom" to make his marriage to Ellen official. There had not even been a minister present who could legally pronounce them man and wife, much less an official ceremony. They were bound together only by their own vows and the desire to love and honor each other all of their lives.

Now, only three generations later, their great-grandson was entering the holy temple to be united in the highest form of marriage with his wife and children, not only for time but for all eternity. Again I felt the tears fall freely as gratitude filled my heart for this blessing. I knew full well that I was preparing to make eternal covenants and commitments and that, even more than before, all of our lives must reflect those covenants.

And as our family participated in the necessary ordinances that morning in the temple, I found that there was one compensation—if you could call it that—for not having been married in the temple originally. It is an exhilarating and eye-opening experience for two parents to have their children, dressed completely in white, walk into the sealing room and kneel beside them at the altar. When our two boys knelt beside us and took our hands, I couldn't help but feel— with a surge of realization—that my children were children of our Heavenly Father, just as I was. Here we knelt together as an earthly family to make eternal covenants that would enable us, if we honored and lived up to those covenants, to return as a family to our Heavenly Father. I've tried to find the words that express how I felt at that moment, but my emotions and feelings go far beyond my ability to express them. I can only give thanks to my Heavenly Father, who loves me.

I walked out of the temple on that sunny day with a recommitment to teach my family the principles of the gospel and the great importance of obedience to those principles. We now had the priesthood to bless our home, and I was determined that we would jump the mortal hurdle together. I would never again have to hand my child over to an elder when it came time to have him or her blessed. Subject to the bishop's approval each time, when my children turned eight I could lead each of them into the waters of baptism and would be the instrument through which each could receive the Holy Ghost. I could preside in my home. My children would be able to be married in the temple, if they lived worthily, and they could rear their families fully within the gospel framework and inside the holy covenant of eternal marriage. To work toward exaltation now seemed a much closer and more realistic goal, for I knew that only within the bonds of eternal marriage could a couple and a family achieve exaltation in the highest realm—godhood. The plan of salvation now fully applied to me— Joseph Freeman, Jr.

I know that the gospel is true. I know that happiness depends on how fully we are willing to live the commandments. It is a tremendously reassuring feeling to know there is one to whom I can always turn for strength, direction, and love—someone who is my Elder Brother, Jesus Christ.

And of course, the feelings and experiences I was having were being duplicated in many other homes. One really tremendous effect of the revelation has been that it has helped not only black members catch the vision of their potential and worth, but it has helped other members and black people all over the world as well. There has been an almost unexplainable increase in love and warmth from members of the Church and an increased interest from nonmembers— particularly black nonmembers.

Our Genesis group has reflected this change. It seems that each week we have new faces in the crowd, and many of the new ones are those who have been contacted by the missionaries and who have then been routed to our group. So far, it has seemed that if a person comes to meet with us more than once, and especially if he comes three times, he eventually joins the Church.

It almost seems that all members of the Church feel an increased desire to fellowship and reach out to black people, whereas prior to the revelation, missionary activity was not particularly directed to the black population and I think Church members in general did not quite know how to deal with the rather awkward Negro/priesthood situation. Now there is no reason for anyone to catch his breath or hesitate when a Negro asks about the Church, for the almost inevitable and embarrassing confrontation does not now have to take place.

There has been a noticeable strengthening among the members of the Genesis group, and we have found that our testimony meetings are even more moving and inspiring than before. I think that we all, as black members of the Church, have a heightened sense of awareness and belonging. After all, it's readily recognized that attitude often determines action. Individuals will usually act or live up to the manner in which they're treated. In other words, if you tell a child that he's smart or clever, chances are he'll really be smart and clever. If you tell your wife what a fine housekeeper she is, she'll work to live up to that praise. We as Negro members of the Church have in essence been reassured that we are now worthy of being treated like everyone else. Self-esteem isn't at the mercy of conditions that can't change. And it has made a difference.

I can feel the change within myself. To know that I've been divinely commissioned to act in the Lord's name evokes simultaneous feelings of self-esteem (my own feelings of worth are enhanced) and humility (can I measure up to this responsibility?). There is a certain sense of pride and a definite thrill that comes with holding and exercising the priesthood. For example, even though I have been a home teacher for several years, whenever my companion and I were called upon to perform an ordinance—administer to the sick, stand in a prayer circle, and so on—my companion always had to call another elder to come with us. I'll always remember the first night that I didn't have to call on another elder to stand in for me. Late in the evening, before I'd come home from work, Toe received a call from friends in the ward who had a young girl visiting them from Hawaii who was very ill. The father needed another priesthood bearer to help him perform the blessing. When I got home at about 11:00 P.M. I went right over to see if they still needed me; as it happened, they did. Their Hawaiian friend had worked herself into a state of exhaustion, was confined to bed, and couldn't perform even the smallest tasks for herself. Her fever was dangerously high, and my worried friends wanted to take her to the hospital. But the girl resisted, insisting that she first have a blessing.

So this other elder and I performed the ordinance. As I pronounced a blessing on her head, I could really differentiate between the simple prayers of faith I'd offered before in behalf of members of my own family and this blessing, which was pronounced according to the will of the Lord and under his specific authority. The words actually came into my mind as I blessed this girl, and I knew that I was speaking for the Lord. It was an overwhelming feeling and experience!

As I spoke, I felt inspired to say that this girl would regain her strength and health. I wasn't prepared for what happened immediately after the blessing, though. She popped up from her chair and hustled to the kitchen to fix punch and cookies for us all. Only ten minutes before she'd lain flat on her back, but now the color had returned to her face, she was up and out of bed, and was even serving us refreshments. I could scarcely believe it! I realized then even more than I had before that the power of the priesthood was not to be underestimated or taken for granted.

Since that time I've stood in the circle as young children have been blessed or confirmed. I have had the opportunity to baptize and ordain. I've pronounced father's blessings upon my children and have administered to my wife in times of illness. I was able to take my second little daughter, who was born in March 1979, in my arms and give her a name and a blessing. I was able to do the same with my adopted daughter. I'm able to work with the young men in our priests quorum as a priest adviser and with other boys as president of the YMMIA. My wife and I enjoy temple sessions together, and I never leave that sacred edifice without feeling uplifted, inspired, and more knowledgeable—and more in love with my eternal companion. In fact, it seems almost selfish to want to go so often—I'm sure I benefit far more than those whose work I'm vicariously participating in. I can preach the gospel to others, knowing full well that if I keep myself worthy the Spirit will attend me as I teach and bear testimony.

A few months after the revelation announcement I lay one evening thinking about all these things, about all the changes the priesthood had made in my life. And it suddenly hit me that my potential is endless. And you know, it really is—for all of us. As members of The Church of Jesus Christ of Latter-day Saints, we have been told by modern prophets that we all have divine potential, that we are gods in embryo. Not only should we be increasingly aware of our heritage and our divine expectations, but we should realize that we have been given all that we need to achieve lofty goals of exaltation.

The phrase coined by Lorenzo Snow—"As man is, God once was; as God is, man may become"—is more than a catchy little couplet: it states simply but accurately our earthly mission. It outlines the expectations our heavenly parents have of us. The Lord instructed Joseph Smith, "Unto whom much is given much is expected." We have been given much; in fact, we have been given all.

I feel burning within myself the challenge to live up to my divine potential. And especially, now that I have felt the power of the priesthood and now that I have seen how the priesthood can bless lives, I know that I must be willing to do everything under my power to achieve exaltation—for it is not some unreachable, unreasonable goal. Exaltation *is*, for each of us, ultimately possible. Lorenzo Snow gave this counsel to priesthood bearers:

> There is just one thing that a Latter-day Saint, an Elder in Israel should never forget: it should be a bright illuminating star before him all the time—in his heart, in his soul, and all through him—that is, he need not worry in the least whether he should be a deacon or President of the Church. It is sufficient for him to know that his destiny is to be like his Father, a God in eternity. He will not only be President but he may see himself president of a kingdom, president of worlds with never-ending opportunities to enlarge his sphere of dominion. (At a meeting of the First Presidency and the Council of the Twelve, recorded in BYU Special Collections, microfilm reel number 1, page 209.)

The Church of Jesus Christ of Latter-day Saints is that bright illuminating star, and is the beacon I look to for guidance. Jesus is the Christ! He died for *my* sins and he stands at the head of his church today. Never have I felt greater peace of mind and joy or had closer communion with the Father than I have since joining the Church.

When I left for Hawaii back in 1972 as an enlisted man in the army, one of my goals was to become rich. At that time I had no idea of the riches I would receive. I feel wealthy beyond measure now, for my membership in the Lord's church, the Holy Melchizedek Priesthood which I hold, and my family whom I love with the purest degree of unconditional love that I have thus far learned to master, have given me the greatest wealth a man could ever hope for.

And should days come when I begin to take all or any of these things for granted, or whenever I get the urge to be a little lax in my obligations and commitments, I'll think of one special experience that will never lose its impact or meaning.

The morning we were sealed in the temple, our two little boys were waiting in the nursery for the time when they'd join us in the sealing room. And of course, little boys will be little boys—even in the temple nursery. I'm sure that after a couple of hours they were getting a little fidgety when finally one of the temple workers told them it was time to go meet their mother and dad. As it was related to us by the temple worker, Alexander immediately snapped to attention. He was ready to go. But Zechariah was playing with something and wasn't hustling quite as fast as his older brother thought he should.

After watching this for a minute or two, Alexander finally said, "Zechariah, come on! We've got to go see Mom and Dad. Don't you know that today we're going to be a family forever?"

And that, to me, says it all.